The Faith of Our Children

The FAITH
of OUR CHILDREN

MARY   ALICE   JONES

ABINGDON PRESS
NEW YORK   •   NASHVILLE

THE FAITH OF OUR CHILDREN

Copyright MCMXLIII by Whitmore & Stone

Scriptural quotations are from the American Standard Version
of the Revised Bible, copyright, 1929, by The International
Council of Religious Education, and are used by permission.

Library of Congress Catalog Card Number: 43-5495

SET UP, PRINTED, AND BOUND BY THE
PARTHENON PRESS, AT NASHVILLE,
TENNESSEE, UNITED STATES OF AMERICA

Preface

"I BELIEVE IN GOD." IN THE HYMNS, THE CREEDS, THE ritual, the prayers of the Christian churches, belief in God is affirmed. In the children's group of the churches and in those homes where the family prays, faith in God is taught. Yet among many teachers there seems to be confusion and a lack of that conviction which is rooted in experience of the reality of God.

Is faith in God important to our children today? And may we encourage them to achieve this faith for themselves in full confidence that it is of the very stuff of reality?

The chapters in this book are written in the hope that they may make some contribution to parents and teachers who wish their children to believe in God, not merely verbally, but in such manner as shall really determine the course of their lives.

It is not a simple assignment to express in language the great affirmations of Christian faith. The writer is aware of many limitations which make it impossible to do as well as it should be done the task which the book has set for itself. Yet it has been undertaken because of the deep conviction, growing out of years of experience in counseling with parents and teachers of children, that they feel the need for some such suggestions as are here outlined. The volume is sent out in the hope, not that it will answer all the questions or give an adequate interpretation to all the difficult problems with which it proposes to deal, but rather in the hope that it will throw a finger of light upon the path and so point the leaders of children toward the need for more adequate resources of insight and wisdom.

These chapters suggest some approaches to guidance for children in the apprehension of God, in the realization of the meaning of salvation in human life, in the appreciation of the resources and the practice of Christian faith. Though in the very nature of the case procedures cannot be separated from purposes, there is no attempt to deal in detail with method. This is due both to limitation of space and to the fact that excellent books in the field of specific procedures and techniques are already available. It is hoped that this book will be used in connection with others, and that they may supplement one another.

In the Curriculum of Leadership Education planned by the denominations co-operating through the International Council of Religious Education there is outlined a comprehensive plan of study for leaders of children of each age group. This includes studies in child nature and how children learn, in the selection and use of materials, and in detailed guidance in the use of effective plans and procedures. For most of these proposed areas of study good textbooks and additional suggested readings are available. The field of the present book is that proposed in the course called "The Child's Approach to Religion."

It would not be possible to acknowledge all the sources from which help has come in planning and preparing the material for this book. In the give and take of conferences with parents and teachers of children in all parts of the country, in the stimulating fellowship of the International Council staff, of the Committee on Religious Education of Children, and of the Children's Work Professional Advisory Section, there has been afforded opportunity for clarification of thoughts and convictions and for illuminating experiences of corporate worship. The members of the faculty and student body of Yale Divinity School have been a source of inspiration and insight, through a period of years as a student and later as a visiting member of the teaching staff. The pulpit of the First Methodist Church in Evanston, Illinois, has supplied much food for thought on all these questions.

To the many writers whose works have been helpful acknowledgment is expressed in the footnotes.

MARY ALICE JONES

Contents

I

The Spiritual Nature of Children

THE QUESTIONS CHILDREN ASK COVER SO WIDE A FIELD that adults are continually surprised, but there are certain questions almost all children ask. In one form or another, every normal child asks how he came to be. From the excellent books and pamphlets and lectures on the subject parents and other teachers have learned some of the helpful and satisfying methods of dealing with this question so far as the biological phases of life are concerned. But many parents do not feel that this answer is a complete answer to their children's questions regarding their creation. They feel that, although a scientific interpretation of life, an interpretation of the *how* of life, so far as it is known and so far as he can understand it, is necessary and helpful to a child, at the same time he needs something more. They are seeking for wise ways of expanding the interpretations to include some suggestions that go back of biological laws and processes into the basic meaning of life itself.

Moreover, the testimony of many parents and teachers indicates that merely the scientific explanation of life does not satisfy the children. They probe beneath it. "If I hadn't been your little girl, who would I have been?" one asks, suggesting that she was struggling with the idea, not of biological creation, but of life as *life*. It was conceivable to her that she might have been someone other than herself, but it was not conceivable that she might not have been at all. "How can God think of me when there are so many things for him to do in the world?" asks another, suggesting that he was sharing something of that sense of wonder expressed by the psalmist:

When I consider thy heavens, the work of thy fingers,
The moon and the stars, which thou hast ordained;
What is man, that thou art mindful of him?

On the other hand, the little boy's question, "Did God remember that you liked curly hair when he planned me?" suggests the child's thought of specific attention, not only to the how of individual creation but to detailed purpose back of it. And the much rarer type of question from children, "Why did God plan people? He had the stars and the flowers," suggests a sense of need for help in interpreting creation on a plane beyond science. Children are philosophers and theologians as well as scientists.

How can we help our children to think intelligently and reverently about their place in the total plan of creation? How can we help them to think about the question of the ages, "What *is* man?"

In the ancient Hebrew writings there is the clear statement: "Ye are the children of the Lord your God," and in the early Christian writings there occur almost the same words: "We are children of God." May we, in our age, teach children this faith and expect them to make it their own? What does it mean?

The Nature of Man

We shall fail in our attempt to interpret life to our children if we assume that this affirmation means they are creatures wholly unrelated to and beyond the rest of creation. We shall fail if we attempt to dodge the fact that man is an animal—a complicated animal, it is true, but an animal none the less. His body is made of the same basic chemical substances as those of other animals. He shares physical needs and appetites with other animals. He fights to preserve his life, to defend his young, to keep his possessions. Often he is "predatory, cruel, deceitful"; and, like all the other animals, he must die.

Since man *is* an animal, parents and teachers should help children to face the fact, as has been suggested, "neither with shame nor with gloating but with candor"; for "to affirm that we are animals is not to deny that we are men." [1] It is rather to understand and be prepared to deal with problems which arise out of one's human nature.

But though he is created of the same basic stuff from which the rest of the universe is made, man is yet different from it. In his little book *What Is Man?* Professor R. L. Calhoun illuminates the point that man alone among earthly creatures evaluates and chooses. Other creatures respond to the laws governing them, without the possibility either of questioning whether this or that is right or of making any choice in the matter. "The seasons come and go, the winds rise and die away, the ocean roars but keeps its appointed place, the plants and animals thrive each after its kind." [2] No one of them makes a moral judgment upon its own activity or the activity of other creatures. Only man decides what is good and chooses to do it.

Man is free to a degree that other forces and other living organisms are not free. By thinking and planning he can, to an important extent, control both his environment and his own impulses and needs. By remembering, he can learn from experience. By the use of imagination he can escape some of the limitations of time and space through putting himself in the place of someone else, in

[1] R. L. Calhoun, *God and the Common Life*, Scribner, 1935, p. 98.
[2] Association Press, 1939, p. 65.

some other country, in some other situation, in some other time. Man is aware of, responds to, and at the same time influences and changes the persons and circumstances and things about him. He can bear in mind the past and the present while he sets for himself future goals. And among the millions of human beings upon the earth each one is different from all the others—individual, unique, "a living soul."

Our children are, then, a part of, and dependent upon, the world about them, but they are also distinct from it. They may understand not only physical facts and forces, but also spiritual realities.

The Price of Freedom

While these privileges lift man above the rest of creation, they also have involved him in serious trouble. For man has misused his high privileges and has willfully sinned against God his Creator.

Man as a morally responsible person has taken his fate into his own hands, and has proved himself unfit for the privilege of freedom. Instead of rising steadily from the animal nature, ... he has mired himself in a "second nature" of individual habits and social customs that hobbles him at every step. . . . . Though still free to think, plan, and choose as other animals are not, he cannot of himself choose as he ought.[3]

Is this, then, man? This creature rooted in animal nature, developed into a second nature of frustration and sin and failure? It is the affirmation of Christian faith that, while man is this, man is more than this. Man was made "in the image of God"—that is, with unique capacity for responding to God, for fellowship with him. With full recognition of man's desperate state, Christian faith can yet

[3] *Ibid.*, p. 69.

12

make the glorious statement: "Beloved, now are we children of God." The Christian's hope lies, not in his own ability to choose aright, to recognize and love and do all things that are good, but rather in God's love for him. This outgoing, creative love of God seeks after man, and "sent his Son" for man's redemption. In the Christian view, man is never for a moment alone, but always, even in his sin, he is with God, "in whose unseen presence he lives and moves and has his being." Man is man because he can be aware of this love and can find full self-realization in responsive love to God and to his fellow men.

The Responsibilities of Sonship

Our children may be taught to think of themselves as the objects of God's thought and care. But they must not be betrayed into assuming that to be children of God is an estate to be lightly regarded. We have often carelessly given our children the impression that it involves no responsibility, no acknowledgment of their dependency upon God, no entering into their sonship. The love of God is active, seeking, limitless: but if man does not respond to it, then may he not fail to realize for himself the place in creation which God intended for him? If he remains insensitive to the love of God as are the seasons, the waves, the winds; if, as Paul says, he "receiveth not the things of the Spirit of God," may he not, indeed, come to be merely a "natural man," a creature among the other creatures of the universe, refusing his birthright as a son of God?

Such men-who-refuse-to-be-men in days of old stirred the pessimistic preacher to say: "That which befalleth the sons of men befalleth beasts; even one thing befalleth them: as the one dieth, so dieth the other." And in the present day the preacher of Ecclesiastes has not a few followers who see man's state as hopeless.

13

It is the affirmation of Christian faith that by recognizing God's love, by responding to it with answering love and service, man becomes a new creature, with power over the "natural man," with unique spiritual endowments and immediate fellowship with God.

Our children are not, then, either "trailing clouds of glory" or mere animals. They are human persons, granted by the Creator the opportunity to rise above the rest of creation, to think God's thoughts after him, to share his purposes, to work with him, to respond to his love. Because of this unique possibility, our children, as persons, are more precious in the thought of God than all the wealth and grandeur and beauty in the physical universe.

To man has been granted the possibility of freedom and power and wisdom beyond all other creatures.

> Thou hast made him but little lower than God,
> And crownest him with glory and honor.
> Thou makest him to have dominion over the works
>   of thy hands;
> Thou hast put all things under his feet.

It is the high privilege of parents and teachers to help children to be aware of their status as *man*, to rejoice in it, to recognize their dependence upon God for it, to be humble in the thought of the confidence God has reposed in them in granting it, and to accept seriously the responsibilities which it lays upon them as children of God.

II

Children's Experience of God

"WHAT AND WHERE IS GOD?" IS THE TITLE OF A WIDELY read and influential book of a few decades ago. And such questions about God, like those concerning their own origin and nature, are asked in one form or another by almost all children. How we long for a simple, concrete answer which we may give them with confidence that it is the *right* answer!

In the very nature of the case, there can be no simple, concrete answer. To questions about God human beings can make no answers which can be proved to be the final and absolutely right answers. "God is great beyond our knowing," and yet we must give our children answers which represent our own best thinking, and help them be able to give a reason for the faith that is in them.

The Contribution of the Home

The preparation of the parent or other teacher to deal with such questions must be made long before the child's questions are asked. In this area we cannot "look up" the answer in the encyclopedia or send the child to the school laboratory or go with him to power plants as we may when he asks questions in the field of history or science or mechanics. Rather, when our children ask questions about God our responses must come out of our own experience, enriched by all that the accumulated wisdom of the race has made available to us. And our responses will be helpful to our children only to the extent that our own experience has been significant to us. If in our own experience God has had no important place, we can, at best, only share with our children an honest doubt. We dare not attempt to share a living faith which we have not experienced.

Long before the child asks his parent any question about God—indeed, before he is capable of using language at all —it is likely that his experiences will have prepared him to share a satisfying faith in God, or will have built barriers in his way to knowing God. For it is clear that adults cannot "teach" children anything unless there is something in the experience of the children which gives the teaching meaning. If they have never known love, wisdom, patience, kindness, these words, when used in answer to questions about God, will convey little meaning to the children. If they have never known orderliness, dependability, consistency in dealing with moral and ethical issues, the description of God as dependable, of his moral law as eternal, will be of little avail. If they have never experienced the joy of creation, if they have never had their attention directed to the cycle of life from a dry, brown seed to a blooming plant, if they have never seen water come bubbling fresh and cool and wholesome from a spring, if they have never watched the sunset turn the windows to gold and the sky to flame, if they have never wondered about the moon and stars—if they have never been made aware of the universe in which they live, it is not likely that the words "God the Father Almighty, Maker of heaven and earth" will be meaningful.

On the other hand, if as little children they have known in their homes love, wisdom, patience, and kindness, boys and girls can build upon these experiences some concept of a God who is altogether loving and wise and patient and kind. If their conduct has been consistently appraised and fairly dealt with, they can begin to understand quite early that the moral order of God is dependable and may not be defied. If they have enjoyed the wonders and beauties in the natural world about them, if they have planted and watered seeds and watched them sprout and blossom, if they have found delight in their color, if they have caught something of the awe and wonder of their adults as they paused silently to watch a sunset or a starry night sky—if in ways such as these, little children have been led to an appreciation of the natural world, gradually the words "Maker of heaven and earth" become increasingly meaningful.

The little child's sense of the reality of God does not, then, come primarily from direct teaching about God, but primarily from sharing experiences of God. If his parents are aware of God and responsive to God, the child will expect to experience God for himself, and so will be more likely to be sensitive to God's presence and God's guidance. "Words may point toward God, but cannot make Him known. He must make Himself known; and only to one who has come to believe himself confronted by God, in the concrete rise and fall of his own living, can such words be more than counters in a mental exercise." [1]

Introducing the Name of God

Just when the word God comes to be associated with some unseen but very real person in the child's thought we cannot be sure. There are those among the careful teachers of little children who advise us to refrain from making direct statements about God to very little children lest they come to substitute words for a real experience. Certainly the many adults around us who speak glibly about God but who confess both in words and in their

---

[1] Calhoun, *God and the Common Life*, p. 241.

lives that they have no real consciousness of God bear witness to the danger of verbal religion as a serious barrier to a vital religion.

Yet it seems scarcely possible, even if it were desirable, in a normal American environment to keep children from hearing God's name mentioned. And so it seems wiser to refer to God by name whenever the occasion arises and to try with each reference to help the little child to grow in understanding. Inevitably he will get some wrong impressions because of his limited experience and language ability. But these need not be serious. He hears references to absent relatives from very early childhood. By the manner in which they are mentioned he gradually builds up some concept of these persons. In similar fashion, if God is real to the adults in his world, references to God will come naturally into conversation and will help the child gradually to build a concept of God.

That this early concept is likely to take the form of a physical person need not permanently limit the child's thought of God provided it is of a good, wise, and loving person. And provided, also, the emphasis in our references to God helps him to think more of the purposes of God and less of the physical form concerning which many little children are curious. To the question, "What does God look like?" we may reply: "God does not need a body like ours. But he loves people. And we know something about how God works and what he does."

Finding Help From the Experiences of Others

But the child is not dependent solely upon his own experience and his own understanding in coming to know God. He may venture out on the experience of others. As has been suggested, those who are close to him and who make it clear in their living as well as in their teaching

18

that to them God is in very truth closer "than breathing, and nearer than hands and feet" will by the testimony of their lives help their children to know God more fully. The Bible record gives a vivid and moving account of the work of God and of how God made himself known to the men of old. The history of the Christian Church also bears witness; and in the great poetry and liturgy, the sacraments and ceremonies of religion are found expressions of the faith of millions of humble men and women of all races and nations to whom the love of God has been the most real experience in life. All these resources are available to us and to our children.

Jesus, the Revelation of God

Supremely in Jesus Christ may our children come to know God. Jesus showed us the Father. Because we may tell our children that God is like Jesus, we may help them to overcome the temptations to worship false gods. In him is made manifest the love of God, the purpose of God for his children. Because we have in the Gospels specific accounts of the way Jesus acted toward persons, we may help our children to know, not in vague generalities, but in concrete detail, how God cares for his children. Because we have the teachings of Jesus, we may help our children to understand how God expects his children to live together, what he expects of them in righteousness and in obedience to his will.

But because Jesus lived on earth at a definite period in history and in a definite country and under definite conditions and customs, there has sometimes arisen confusion when parents and teachers have interpreted Jesus to boys and girls as the revelation of God. They have come to think of God as operating under the same limitations which Jesus assumed during his earthly life. This misunderstanding we must seek to avoid. Jesus, who lived among men, showed them God in his relationships with men—as one who loved them and drew them to himself in responding love and obedience, as the righteous judge who required righteousness among men and upheld moral law. But Jesus assumed no powers as Creator or Sustainer of the Universe. Though Jesus lived under the limitations of human knowledge, God is omniscient; though Jesus lived under the limitations of human strength, God is omnipotent; though Jesus lived under the limitations of time and space, God is omnipresent.

The Initiative of God

In all our teaching we work in the faith that God is not passively waiting to be "found" by his children. He takes the initiative; he is continuously seeking to make himself known. Just how God makes himself known to human personalities we may not say. He works in many ways. Sometimes knowledge of God comes gradually as life unfolds. To some persons God reveals himself primarily in striking splendor through the beauty of the earth. To some he becomes known through quiet meditation as the meaning of experience becomes clear. To some God speaks in illuminating moments of mystical communion as spirit meets spirit. To some God seems most real in corporate worship; to some, in harmonious human fellowship. But in all these experiences God is active, God takes the initiative.

Some present-day theologians are laying stress indeed, not only upon the initiative of God but also upon the absolute "otherness" of God. In their view, God does not—cannot—make himself known through nature or through the experiences of men because God is wholly *"other than"* nature and man. Rather, God "breaks through" nature and experience. Says Emil Brunner:

The mysterious God, whom the world neither knows nor shows, whom I do not know and whom the inner man does not reveal . . . . must assert himself over against the world as a being who is not-world, not-ego; who reveals his true name, the secret of his unknown will which is opposed to the world, contrary to our experience and, above all, to the thoughts and intents of our own heart.[2]

While our emphasis has been upon a different view of God's activity in making himself known to his children, this view suggests a needed corrective. We would be misleading children if we taught them to limit their expectation of being confronted by God solely to his revelation in nature, in their own life experiences, in the experiences of others, and even in what we can understand of the earthly experience of Jesus. God does "break through" into the world in ways past our finding out; he does hide from the wise and reveal to the foolish his ways. He does "break through" the limitations of previous human experience and become known in a sudden flash of insight. He does "break through" nature and make himself known in spite of disharmony and destruction. "Nature . . . . is in process of being brought into accord with the demands of 'what ought to be'—in process of being 'reconciled'— rather than already exemplifying perfectly the will of God." [3]

The present world order is not God. Men—all men— fall far short of their high calling. Neither in nature nor in human relationships may we lead our children to expect to see God fully revealed. Yet in nature and in human relationships we find clues to the nature and the purposes of God. Though they are far from what they ought to be,

---

[2] Emil Brunner, *Theology of Crisis*, Scribner, 1929, p. 31.

[3] Calhoun, *God and the Common Life*, p. 247.

they are not wholly other than, apart from, God. Rather, we may with confidence assume that, they give us an imperfect reflection of God's great and good purposes, now but dimly realized yet in process of being realized.

In the literature of religion there are countless records of God's revelation of himself to man. To attempt to limit, or even to describe, the manner or the occasion of God's revelation of himself to any child is not the province of a teacher. It is the opportunity of the teacher to lead the child to expect that God will make himself known and to be sensitive to God's revelations of himself whenever they come.

The Need for Direct Teaching

One's understanding of God, one's ideas of God, then, are rooted in the experience of being "confronted by God" in one's own life, in nature, in human relationships, in history, and in Jesus Christ. But children need also the clarification of experience and definite suggestion and explication regarding thoughts of God and of his purposes.

Vague, diffuse "feelings" of God may become dissipated or lead to unwholesome attitudes. Growing children need help in expressing their faith and thereby clarifying it and strengthening it. Through wise guidance as they wonder and question, through fellowship in worship with others, through voicing their yearnings and aspirations in prayer, through specific and careful teaching about God, growing boys and girls may be helped to enrich and interpret their experience of God.

There is also a place for definite correction when the teacher finds that the child is harboring a conception of God which is out of harmony with the Christian view of God and of his purposes. A child who is terrified lest God strike him dead with a bolt of lightning because of some misdeed needs to be told promptly that God is not like that. More often, however, childish misconceptions may most effectively be dealt with indirectly by suggesting thoughts or planning experiences which point in a more satisfying direction.

Right thoughts of God will be helpful, too, as children seek to understand how God speaks to them. They must learn to distinguish between the voice of God and the voice of selfish ambition, between the guidance of God and the natural impulses to assert themselves, between the "quickening of the Spirit" and hysterical excitement. Children have direct access to God: they do not have to approach him through human intermediaries. But parents and teachers may make a great contribution to their children by helping them to interpret their experiences and by suggesting ways in which they may hear God speak to them.

The Importance of the Teacher's Own Faith

This brings us to the importance of right concepts of God on the part of adults. Parents and teachers of children need a sound theology! A great deal of distress is caused many children and growing boys and girls, not because they have misunderstood what has been said about God, but because they have understood and the adult statement rested on an unsound theology. Many parents and other teachers have merely accepted what has been taught them about God and, uncritically, have passed it on to their children without any real experience of it or understanding of it. In such cases they are not sharing a living faith, but they are merely transmitting a creed or a set of ways-of-behaving or of things-that-are-not-done or of doctrines-others-have-taught-me.

This need not be a hypocritical procedure. The teachers are not telling children something which they themselves have rejected. They have not rejected it. Neither have they adopted it. They have passively accepted it without

23

making it a part of their ongoing thinking or purposing or living. It seems to be true, as Dr. E. Stanley Jones has said, that many Christians would be equally shocked to hear their professed creeds doubted and to see them put into practice.

The result of this passive—even though devout—attitude toward religious teachings and practices has been serious in the lives of many alert boys and girls. They are taught in school to think, to question, to find out why, to experiment. They attempt to bring this inquiring attitude into the field of their religious teachings, and they find that their parents or teachers—or even pastors—are either shocked by hearing questions raised or unprepared to deal with them. This response of their teachers often leads first to confusion, and then to secret scepticism, and then to indifference toward religious teachings.

These boys and girls are not satisfied merely by resort to quotations from the creed or from the prayer book or even from the Bible. They want to think for themselves about the questions which have arisen in their minds. They want to explore new ideas. They want to probe beneath beautiful phrases to find what they mean in terms of the here and now as well as in terms of eternity. Then they will welcome creeds, prayer books, and Bible readings to correct and enrich their thinking.

Parents and teachers must, then, be able to give a reason for the faith that is in them. And they must teach theology if they are to teach children. They must be prepared to meet inquiring minds with sympathy for the inquiry and with knowledge and experience and useful materials with which to guide them forward toward positive conclusions.

This requires that they know the Bible and how to use it in teaching children. Often carelessly told Old Testament

24

stories, for example, give children a wrong concept of God which, because it bears the prestige of a Bible story, is especially hard to correct. Stories which represent God as vengeful, cruel, capricious; as commanding the slaughter of men and beasts after a victory over an enemy army; as sending out bears to devour children who venture to jest at a prophet—such stories create many problems in the religious development of children and should not be told. There will come a time in the child's development when he has a background of history which will help him to interpret these early conceptions of God; but while he is a child, only those stories from the Old Testament should be selected which help clarify the child's thoughts of God in harmony with the teachings and revelation of Jesus.

In no other literature is the consciousness of God so vividly portrayed as in the Bible. To the ancient Hebrews God was the most real and the most important fact of life. In him they lived and moved and had their being. To search the Scriptures for insight and inspiration, and to teach our children so to do, is one of the most helpful of all our approaches to knowing God and understanding his purposes for men.

Again, the necessity of teaching theology requires that thoughtful scrutiny be given to all the materials used in worship, especially the songs and prayers, to insure a Christian interpretation of God and his purposes. Frequently songs are used which reflect a positively pagan idea of God and which express aspirations far from those of Jesus. All such materials definitely hinder the child's understanding of God's purposes.

When we say parents and teachers must have a sound theology and must teach theology to children, we do not mean there is one absolutely right and wholly adequate concept of God which must be taught to children in authoritative terms. No two persons are likely ever to have exactly the same concept of God because no two persons ever have exactly the same needs or experiences. And the doctrinal catechism of questions and answers about God is not generally regarded as the most helpful approach by which a child comes to know God. But it seems clear that everyone who considers religion an important part of living should learn to worship God with his *mind* as well as with his heart. He should *know* whom he has believed.

The results of our interpretation of experience and our direct teaching about God will be tested, not by the child's ability to give right answers to questions about God, but by his growing desire and ability to respond to God, to live as a child of God. Our children must understand that no human being is likely ever fully to understand God and his purposes. But neither is any human being likely to grow in understanding of God until he begins to try to live in accordance with the purposes of God for men. It is contrary to all that we know of God's ways with men to assume that God grants a growing knowledge of himself to men who take no account of that knowledge which has already been vouchsafed to them. Rather, as one lives in accordance with the light which he has, greater light will come; as he ventures out in fellowship with God to do his will, growing appreciation of the purposes and of the methods of God will come to him.

The following chapters will attempt to interpret more in detail the point of view which has been here presented.

III

The Love of God

THE LITTLE CHILD EARLY LEARNS TO ASSOCIATE THE word "love" with care and protection and provision for physical needs. He is told that his mother loves him, and it is to his mother he looks for attention when he is uncomfortable, for food when he is hungry, for care when he is hurt. He hears it said that his father loves him, and it is to his father that he comes to look for security from want and for protection from danger. So when the little child hears references to the love of God, he associates it readily with material care, physical comforts, personal attention, and protection.

Love Revealed in Provision for Physical Need

Probably this is inevitable. It may also become a useful approach in teaching children. One has to make a *beginning* in theology as in anything else, and the normal beginning point for a theology may well be the experience of love expressed through provision for daily needs. So we may call attention to the provision in the natural world of fruits and vegetables and grains for food; to the provision of day and night for work and play and rest; to the provision of families for the nurture of children; to the provision of beauty for the joy and happiness of all men. We may help the little child to be increasingly aware of these evidences of God's love, and through them to come to know that God has planned a beautiful, fruitful, and good world for his children, and to find delight in it.

Beginning in quite earthy terms, how may we help the little child, as he grows in stature, to grow also in his understanding of God's love? Perhaps one of the most serious handicaps in our teaching at this point has been our reluctance to let the child grow! We have wished to shelter him from life as it is. Consequently, we have not been willing to consider with him how God's love operates in the world when the interest of one man or nation collides with the interest of another, or when the beneficence of nature is turned into destruction, or when the accumulation of power and possessions, rather than the nurture of persons, comes to be regarded as the mark of human greatness. And so in his theology he continues to think as a child while in his science and his mechanics and his history he has become a man. Long after he should have put away childish things, he continues to think of God's love only in terms of personal care and protection and pleasure. Then he meets life as it is, real life. Disaster comes; sorrow engulfs him; disappointment crushes him. And in all of this what he has learned of the love of God seems a mockery.

The Love of God and Man's Sin

Is the love of God for a man or a nation to be measured by comfort and prosperity and protection from ills? Are suffering and disaster evidences that God's love has been withdrawn because of man's disloyalty or sin?

The Old Testament wise men taught that there is a clear connection between the favor of God and prosperity. This teaching was based on the thought that Israel stood in a covenant relation to Jehovah: Israel must obey the laws of Jehovah, and Jehovah would protect and reward Israel. In the Proverbs this doctrine is very explicit. The rewards offered the righteous man may be condensed into a short list, comprehensive of the desires of the people of that day: life, health, honor, peace, a large family, and revenge upon enemies. Also, in the view of the sages of old, God gave expression to righteous wrath when man failed to be obedient. The punishments for evil are as sure and as explicit as are the rewards for virtue: death, pain, poverty, shame, a dying family tree, hatred and strife.[1]

The great prophets rose above this interpretation and taught that the love of God overflowed legal barriers—that without regard to man's deserts the love of God would not let him go, would follow him even through degradation and sin with redemptive fellowship. "I have loved thee with an everlasting love"; "I will heal their backsliding, I will love them freely."

In the thought of Jesus, there is recognition for those who are loyal to God's purposes—recognition expressed in terms of participation in the Kingdom of God. But the emphasis in his teaching is upon the love of God, which is bestowed, not because man merits it, but because it is of the nature of God to love his children. It is out-going, seeking love. This does not mean that man may transgress the moral laws of God with impunity. The prodigal son sinned, and he suffered. But his sin did not turn away the love of the father: the love of the father went forth to meet the son while he was yet afar off. It was not a measured, cautious love, waiting to make sure that the sinner was penitent, that he would never again sin; it was generous, boundless, joyous love which had never for a moment wavered, which had been always ready, which was eagerly looking for the son, which welcomed him without reserve.

[1] Paul S. Minear, *And Great Shall Be Your Reward*, Oxford, 1941, p. 4.

In some Christian teaching there has been injected the thought that God does not love those who refuse to accept his purposes. Even on superficial examination this doctrine must be discredited. Yet it has persisted. The human analogy should reveal its falseness: do parents turn away from the child who refuses to co-operate in plans for the family happiness and welfare? Do they cease to love the child who sins against them? The cases in which they do are so rare as to become noteworthy. Even when their evil-doings bring public disgrace and cause immeasurable anguish of spirit, most children can depend upon the continuing, yearning love of their parents. Jesus taught explicitly that *men* were to love those who were unloving, unfriendly, abusive. How much more shall God love those who fail him! However much God opposes evil, it is a cardinal affirmation of the Christian faith that he loves and seeks the sinner. "While we were yet sinners," Paul testifies, "God commendeth his own love toward us" and sent his son to die for us. Let no Christian teacher be guilty of saying to a child, "If you do that, God will not love you!" No statement could be more profoundly untrue.

Love Experienced in Fellowship

If the love of God embraces the sinner as well as the saint, may not the child who is loyal to his Father's will expect an added measure of his thought and bounty? The life of Jesus makes it abundantly clear that no such special favors may be expected, that the love of God is not expressed through such rewards. Jesus was wholly devoted to the will of God. Yet he had not where to lay his head; he was despised and rejected of men; he suffered as few men have suffered; he died the death of a criminal. In his life and in his death Jesus repudiated the doctrine that God's love would insure to his loyal children

30

prosperity, special benefits, special exemptions from the ills of life.

Rather, Jesus interpreted the love of God in terms of fellowship. "I am not alone, because the Father is with me." Fellowship was to Jesus the true measure of God's love. Because God was with him, he could endure hardships, suffer torture, see his dreams fade around him, and accept the desertion of his friends without despair. Indeed, in spite of all these experiences, his message is essentially a message of joy. Throughout long days in the desert, during the nights on the mountain, in the grueling hours of his trial, as well as in moments spent in happy human comradeship and in enjoying the beauty of flowering meadows, Jesus experienced fellowship with God. His confidence in God and in God's love, even when all external evidences of it were removed from him, came from his experience of God. He *knew* God. And because he knew him, he knew that the love of God was real and abiding and active, making for goodness and joy though suffering and evil were about him.

It is this high concept of the love of God which we wish our children to develop and in which we wish them to find abiding happiness. May we expect them to move from the *beginning* thought of the love of God revealed in terms of physical comforts and benefits to the concept of the fellowship of God, supporting them, giving meaning and purpose to their struggle to achieve their full stature as sons of God? The Christian faith affirms that we may. But we shall be disappointed in our expectations if we fail to help our children to face life as it is even while they are children and to experience the love of God even in the midst of conditions and situations which ignore it.

Of course, in its fullness, this conception of the love of God is a mature conception. It will have increasing meaning as one meets the varied situations of life, with its misunderstandings and frustrations and loneliness as well as its moments of glorious fulfillment and happiness. We may not expect boys and girls to move rapidly from the thought of God as the Great Provider to the thought of God as the Great Companion, and we shall make a mistake if we attempt to hurry them along.

And yet we shall make a greater mistake if we fail to recognize that the sense of fellowship is very real to a child and that it is the experience upon which we may build with the greatest confidence. The children in England during the terrible bombing raids made it very clear that we have underestimated the significance of this experience. The reports show that children can stand up under physical deprivation and danger far better than they can stand up under a sense of separation from those who love them and that they can undergo an amazing amount of hardship provided they are in close contact with their parents.

Phyllis Bottome in her book *London Pride* gives a picture of this situation. The book is a narrative of the struggles and the heroism of one of London's dockland families during the days of the most intense air war. The family was poor, an "underprivileged family" we should say, before the war. Now even the little they had seemed about to be taken away. Poor as it was, they had had a home. Now they slept in a crowded shelter. Ben, a little boy of seven, is the central figure in the narrative. And the writer describes his feelings in this fashion:

His family had assumed a quite surprising importance to him; . . . . somehow the whole family seemed nearer together because of their threatened home. . . . . When his father was not there he noticed the guns more; and when the near crashes came, followed by the eerie silence of disaster, Ben caught his breath till his chest ached, he so much wanted *not* to hear the crackling sound that came a moment later to tell him that a house was burning—perhaps their own. But if his father was there, he just snuggled closer against him and knew that, since the regular quiet beats of the heart he was leaning against did not change, there wasn't much to worry about.[2]

It seems clear from the evidence which we now have that even very little children are much more aware of the sense of fellowship than we had thought and that we may begin quite early to interpret the love of God in these terms. Moreover, let us not limit too narrowly the basis in human relationships of this feeling of fellowship. Again the experience of the children of London throws light upon the problem. It was not only through caresses and tenderness and bounty that the sense of belonging was developed. Many of the evacuated children actually pined for scuffings from rough fathers, teasing from older brothers, scoldings from tired mothers! Under all this they had felt the sense of belonging, which was more precious to them than any amount of comfort. Some children who, from external view, appeared to have little in their lives to form a basis for understanding and valuing fellowship were found to have a very real sense of belonging. These facts suggest that the thought of God's love as finding expression primarily through fellowship may be more meaningful to children than dependence upon its manifestations in terms of physical care and security.

Helping Children to Show Love to Others

It is also becoming increasingly clear that overindulgent parents and teachers who attempt to protect their children from facing life as it is and meeting it squarely may

---

[2] Little, Brown & Co., 1941.

be actually putting barriers in the way of their children's understanding of God's love and purposes. By keeping the attention of children upon their own needs, by allowing them to be always on the receiving end of generosity and kindness and unselfishness, such parents and teachers are depriving their children of opportunity to experience the giving side of love; and this limits their ability to understand the outgoing, creative love of God.

Among the Hebrew prophets it was Hosea, who had himself experienced love which suffered for and reclaimed a wife who had betrayed him, love which would not accept denial—it was Hosea who most clearly interpreted the long-suffering love of God for a wayward people. Jesus, who loved his fellow men as none other has loved them, was the supreme interpreter of the love of God to men. Through the ages the men and women who have been most helpful to others in understanding the love of God have been those who have loved their fellows unselfishly, without reserve, and this in spite of the fact that more often than not their love has caused them suffering. Paul, Francis of Assisi, Florence Nightingale, and thousands of unknown disciples have thus participated in spreading abroad the love of God.

It seems clear that if we wish our children to grow in knowledge of the love of God we must help them to grow in experience of outgoing love. As soon as they can begin to distinguish between "me" and "others," children may be given opportunities to plan for others. At first, very little will be expected. Little children are centered in themselves and need to become aware of themselves. But by hearing reference to other persons, to what they like, to what pleases them, gradually there comes to the little child an awareness of other persons toward whom he stands in the relationship of giving as well as the relationship of receiving. By making the early relationship of giving a happy, satisfying one we may increase the likelihood that it will be strengthened.

As the child grows older, there will come occasions when he must make a choice between pleasing himself and pleasing others. Such occasions should not always be resolved by devoted parents in favor of pleasing himself. And the choice to please others should be allowed to stand on its own merits: there should be no artificial reward attached to it.

This growing experience of love from the giving end will lead almost always into some situations where one must suffer for love's sake. Perhaps the one beloved is in pain or sorrow. Perhaps he is unhappy, frustrated. Perhaps he even betrays the love, or laughs at it, or is found unworthy of trust. To help boys and girls to face such experiences and to come through them with a deeper understanding of the meaning of love offers the parent and teacher an opportunity to make a lasting contribution to the growth of the child's personality. And along with this developing experience of love, the child may gradually come to know that God's love for him is not bounded by security and comfort. He may not understand why there are disasters and struggle and suffering, but neither will he feel that they deny the love of God.

The Love of God and Suffering

There is a large measure of suffering in the world which we can say with complete confidence is contrary to the will of God. The suffering of men, women, and children caused by greed, careless disregard of the rights of others, selfish ambition; the hunger and cold and loneliness of little children caused by social injustice, racial prejudice, or economic malpractice; the ravages of diseases, easily controlled or eliminated when the resources of science are made available—suffering resulting from causes such as these we know to be contrary to the loving purposes of God.

Suffering due to obvious violations of the laws of health and accidents which are the direct result of refusal to observe the laws of safety, even though they result in suffering for the innocent victims, can nevertheless be faced without involving insurmountable difficulties in the way of faith in the goodness and love of God. In all these situations children can be helped to understand that human selfishness, ignorance, carelessness, are working contrary to the good purposes of God and that, because of the measure of freedom which has been granted mankind, they cannot be ejected forcibly from the scheme of things.

But what shall we say of floods, of tempests, of famine, of drought? Children are aware of the terrible results of these forces and ask questions about them. At this point we must confess to our children the limitations of our knowledge. There are not yet enough data available for us to be able to speak regarding the cause and the control of natural disasters. However, only a few years ago we knew nothing about the generation and the control of electrical current. No doubt the early explorers thought waterfalls and rapids were unmitigated evils, blocking their progress, causing them danger and delay. Now we know how to harness these forces to light our homes and drive the machinery of production. A few years ago we knew nothing about the control of sound waves. Now we have the radio. While new discoveries of age-old laws of the universe are crowding upon one another in such rapidity, how can we know that certain natural forces which seem to us in our present ignorance to be bad will not, as our knowledge broadens, be seen as sources of beauty and joy?

In the presence of barriers of nature and of disasters is it reasonable, then, to invite our children to join us in an affirmation of faith that beyond our present knowledge there is a good purpose which these forces, when they are fully understood, are destined to serve? We believe that we may confidently invite such an affirmation when we join with it a reverent determination to learn more of the nature of the universe that we may discover this purpose and help to realize it.

But we may be asked: Why could not other provision for electrical current have been made by an all-wise and all-good Creator than one which involved hardship for mankind? Even though natural forces which now bring disaster will some day be brought under control for good, why was the world made so that there had to be suffering before man learned how to control them? These questions cannot be ignored. And yet, again we shall have to confess the limitation of our knowledge—a limitation of knowledge of what is required to bring men and women to their highest development, to help them to achieve their noblest destiny, to develop all their latent potentialities.

Even little children can understand that when everything they want is handed to them without any effort on their part, they fail to enjoy themselves. The play which they find most agreeable is that which involves effort on their part, discovery, creativity, the stretching of muscles until they are tired. It seems clear from the history of the race that the greatest among men have been those who have achieved as the result of struggle. Is it not, then, reasonable to suggest to boys and girls who raise such questions that probably man needed to make strenuous efforts to discover and control natural forces in order that he might become the sort of person who could enjoy, and appreciate, and look forward to, larger achievements?

A little child knows that some things must be borne for the sake of others of larger value. He does without an ice-cream cone today that he may accumulate a fund to buy a ball tomorrow. He refrains from the second piece of pie because he wants to feel well tomorrow. He understands, though dimly perhaps, that his parents do not suggest that he deny himself either the ice-cream cone today or the second piece of pie because they do not love him but because they want him to have a larger good.

We do not yet fully know the place of struggle and suffering in human life. As has been said, some causes of suffering among men we know to be contrary to the purposes of God. But whether there is an indispensable role which some suffering plays in the development of human personality we may not say. We may not be blind to the fact that many of the world's great personalities, indeed, the greatest of them, have been those who have borne a large degree of suffering. Neither may we ignore the evidence that many persons have come out of experiences of suffering, stronger and kinder persons. It is important, therefore, in helping our children to come to an abiding knowledge of the love of God that we face with them the fact of suffering and help them to achieve the faith that suffering is not "visited upon" persons because God is angry with them. Suffering does not separate men from God's companionship.

Perhaps this seems a somber interpretation of the love of God for little children. Certainly we must not allow adult experience of frustration and suffering and distress to overshadow little children. "Yea, though I walk through the valley of the shadow of death, I will fear no evil, for thou art with me"—this is not the normal approach of the little child to an understanding of God's love. But within the child's own experience are coming experiences of suffering. A dearly loved pet dies in spite of devoted care; flowers that have been planted and tended with joy and faithfulness fade and wither under some blight or drought; a baby bird falls from its nest and is found crushed on the ground. Such experiences cannot be ignored in the life of children.

Thus, though the fact of suffering must be faced, we must bear in mind that for his spiritual growth, as for his physical well-being, the little child needs to be kept in the sunlight, not thrust into the shadows. It is our responsibility as the mature members of a community to provide for our children as large a measure of security and happiness as through our best efforts we are able to provide for them. The beauties of the earth, the joy of human love, the satisfactions of a sturdy body and an alert mind—these experiences we shall lift up so that our children may sense in them the love and the good purposes of God for all his children. The amazing fact about the world is not that there is some ugliness and evil and suffering in it but that there is so much of beauty and goodness and joy.

"Is the universe friendly?" is the basic question which men have asked through the ages. Are the struggles, the suffering, the aspirations of man related to good purposes for him; or is the universe coldly indifferent to man, as a great road machine is indifferent to the crawling life which it crushes in its path? The Christian faith affirms that at the heart of the great universe there is God, who is love. Because God does care, because the universe is friendly, suffering may be borne bravely as an attendant

39

circumstance—often not understood—of the great purpose of a loving God.

To be able to feel that God *is* love, to help children to associate joy and beauty and physical provisions with God's care, and at the same time to be able to face with them the fact that suffering, struggle, and want must also be compassed in God's love, is to achieve the faith and courage worthy of truly Christian teachers.

IV

The Greatness of God

THE NATURAL WORLD, FROM THE TIME OF THE earliest records, has aroused awe and wonder, fear and worship in the heart of man. Power which he could not control, sustenance without which he could not live, life which he could not create, all made him know that he was dependent upon, and at the mercy of, the phenomena which he observed. And so, in one manner or another, all the tribes of men have developed some conception of the Great Cause and some procedures for getting in touch with the power which they experienced but could not direct. Some of these conceptions are crude, even revolting, to modern man. Some of them seem childish or silly. Some of them are noble.

The ancient Hebrews have left us in an inspiring literature, the record of their growing understanding of the source of being and of power, Jehovah, the great God above all gods. In this literature there are evidences of fear and misunderstanding and primitive mores. But against this background, the strength and beauty of the faith of the Hebrews in Jehovah have been so compelling that men of every race and nation have found in the literature of the Old Testament a source of confidence in the reality of God and of insight into his nature and his purposes.

One of the outstanding contributions of the Hebrews to the religious development of mankind is their assurance of the greatness of Jehovah. "O Jehovah my God, thou art very great"—this was the constant affirmation. "Great is Jehovah, and greatly to be praised; And his greatness is unsearchable"; "Thou, Jehovah, art most high above all the earth: Thou art exalted far above all gods"; "The everlasting God, Jehovah, the Creator of the ends of the earth, fainteth not, neither is weary"; "Thou rulest over all; and in thy hand is power and might."

Greatness as Power

Nothing could stand against this power, and the people whose God was Jehovah had a tremendous advantage over all the peoples who did not know him. The vivid story of Elijah, the prophet of Jehovah, challenging the prophets of Baal to a contest of power before all the people symbolizes the thought of the might of Jehovah in contrast with that of any other god. Said Elijah, "Call ye on the name of your god, and I will call on the name of Jehovah: and the God that answereth by fire, let him be God."

Mighty in battle was Jehovah, and his people were never defeated when they obeyed his rules. A handful of soldiers with pitchers and trumpets and torches, who acknowledged Jehovah as their God, put to flight a host of the Midianites. A shepherd boy with a sling and a stone, who went forth "in the name of Jehovah of hosts, the God of the armies of Israel," was mightier than a giant clad in full armor, who served the Philistine gods. Confidence in the power of Jehovah was the source of courage and hope, even against heavy odds.

The Creation of Beauty

While the Hebrews thus ascribed unto Jehovah might and power over all enemies, they early showed also a unique sensitiveness to the greatness of God as revealed in beauty and grandeur and the cycle of the seasons and provision for the needs of men. The starry heavens, the unwearied sun, seedtime and harvest, day and night, the mountains round about Jerusalem and the well-watered valleys, called forth awe and wonder and were expressed in psalms of praise:

> O Jehovah my God, thou art very great;
> Thou art clothed with honor and majesty:
> Who coverest thyself with light as with a garment;
> Who stretchest out the heavens like a curtain;
> Who layeth the beams of his chambers in the waters;
> Who maketh the clouds his chariot;
> Who walketh upon the wings of the wind; . . . .
> Who laid the foundations of the earth,
> That it should not be moved for ever. . . . .
> The earth is filled with the fruit of thy works. . . . .
> O Jehovah, how manifold are thy works!
> In wisdom hast thou made them all.

Contemplation of the world led to thoughts of creation and to the noble expression of the power and work of God found in the first chapter of Genesis: "In the beginning God created the heavens and the earth."

The Majesty and Holiness of God

In the literature of the Old Testament, Jehovah is exalted, full of glory. Men did not approach him lightly but stood in reverence before him. In the vision of Isaiah he saw the Lord "sitting upon a throne, high and lifted up; and his train filled the temple." Seraphim stood about him, crying, "Holy, holy, holy, is Jehovah of hosts: the whole earth is full of his glory." Isaiah was overwhelmed by the vision of the majesty and the holiness of God. "Woe is me!" he said, "for I am undone; because I am a man of unclean lips, and I dwell in the midst of a people of unclean lips: for mine eyes have seen the King, Jehovah of hosts."

Jehovah's power was from everlasting to everlasting; it reached high as heaven and deep as Sheol; and gradually the Hebrews learned to know that it extended to the ends of the earth and overshadowed all men as Jehovah "looketh forth upon all the inhabitants of the earth."

This conception of the greatness of God had a profound influence upon the life and history of the Hebrew people and through them upon the history of the world. Before it the conception of idle pleasure-loving gods who shared the impulses and sins of their worshipers could not stand, and the gods who could be cajoled or forced to do man's will lost their power. "I am God, and not man," the prophet reported; and in accepting this word as the cornerstone of their faith, the Hebrew people gave mankind the basis of high religion.

At the same time, this emphasis upon the holiness, the otherness of God tended toward the development of a large element of fear in worship, the establishment of rigid ceremonials for getting in touch with him. Through the great prophets and especially through the life and teachings of Jesus there came about a modification which enabled simple men and women to approach God as their father, without elaborate rules and rites. Man's awe came to be tempered by confidence in the care of God for his children and so to be less overwhelming. This tendency toward emphasis upon the approachableness of God has increased until it, in its turn, needs modification.

Teaching the Greatness of God

It seems clear that present-day religious education in most of the churches assumes free access to God, the yearning of God to welcome his children into fellowship with him, and the confidence that God depends upon the cooperation of his children for the realization of his purposes

44

in the world. And all this, we feel, is sound assumption. But there is also evidence that there has been too little emphasis upon the holiness, the greatness, the otherness of God, and too much emphasis upon man's own sufficiency. When a group of young people can, in seriousness, raise a banner bearing the words, "Courage God, we come!" there can be no doubt that we should reconsider our emphases. And when there come in from almost every conference with teachers and parents of children illustrations of prayers in which there has been evident the assumption that God would adjust his cosmic purposes to suit the convenience, or to meet the aspirations—or even to set aside the consequences of neglect—of some of his children, it seems clear that we should re-examine our teachings.

In our eagerness to help children to feel at home in their world, to feel secure in the thought of the fellowship of God, we have interpreted the greatness of God almost exclusively in terms of his plans for a beautiful world for the pleasure of his children and a fruitful world for their nurture. The strong emphasis upon the power and the might and the majesty and the holiness of God, so prominent in the literature of the ancient Hebrews, we have neglected. And this neglect has limited seriously the helpfulness of our teaching. Belief in God the Father Almighty, has been taught to boys and girls in the words of the creed; but there has been little emphasis upon it in the total program. The "Father Almighty, Maker of heaven and earth," may not be the object of careless worship or casual affection.

We need not be bound by the Hebrew's interpretation of the way God's power is expressed; we need not repeat Elijah's experiment on Mount Carmel. But if, in our rejection of the limitations in these early expressions of the greatness of God, we reject also the eternal truth that *God is very great*, that God is the supreme power in the universe, that his sovereignty may not be challenged, we shall be limiting seriously our children's understanding of God.

Probably the first approach to an understanding of the greatness of God is through the world of nature. For little children, the ugly bulb that becomes a beautiful flower, the seed that becomes a nourishing vegetable, the stars in the night sky, the rainbow against a cloud all call forth wonder and awe; and these feelings may be cultivated. The perfection of little things, the delicate balance of a butterfly's wing, the color of a tiny wild flower, the pattern of leaves—these also offer opportunity for building a response to the greatness of God.

Older boys and girls need increased contact with the grander, sterner aspects of God's creative power. The vast movements of the planets, towering mountain peaks, the surging sea, the roar of cataracts pouring over sheer cliffs age after age, the raging force of a tempest—these all speak of the power of the Creator, power that is limitless, incomprehensible to man's mind—power before which he trembles, realizing his own littleness and impotence and ignorance.

The transcendent sovereignty of God we need to interpret to boys and girls. God *is*. Whatever man may do or fail to do, God is the same yesterday, today, and forever. To be confronted by God is a tremendous experience. It may not be lightly regarded. Professor Van Dusen calls attention to this fact:

If there be a God, he cannot be one among other more or less interesting factors in the Universe. Rather he must be the one primal and supremely significant fact—in relation to which all others must be oriented and given their significance. Only when we so think of him are we thinking of God. By the same token, if religion be man's relation to that unique and primal Reality, it *must* be a matter of central and utterly unique concern. If we think of it as a quite casual affair, or if we in fact grant it an accidental importance in life, it is not RELIGION with which we have to do, but some cheap and inconsequential counterfeit.[1]

"Be still and know that I am God" is counsel which well may be applied in present-day religious teaching. Children have been too often led into a false conception of life and of the universe by the careless attitudes toward God and toward religion on the part of their elders and, also, by interpreting God solely in terms of human ideals. We have assumed that our ways are God's ways and our thoughts, his thoughts. Yet it now is clear that any interpreter who seeks to *identify* God with our own social movements, however promising they may seem, will be, as Karl Barth said, profoundly embarrassed. To help our children to recognize that God is "great beyond our knowing" is as important a part of our responsibility as to teach them that God is near to each one of them. To help them to recognize, and stand in awe before, his sovereign power is as important as to help them to know that they may go to him in confidence as a child approaches his father.

Man's Response to the Power of God

But God is not mere power. There is purpose, wisdom, mercy, as well as power in the acts of God. Boys and girls must be taught to know that because God is God and not man, there is much in the world which they are not able to understand. But at the same time, it is not man's lot merely to stand in reverent awe in the presence

---

[1] H. P. Van Dusen, *God in These Times*, Scribner, 1935, pp. 68-69.

of God's power. Rather, it is the teaching of Jesus that God's sovereignty is now in action, God's power is operating in men, through men, and for men. To trust this power, to receive it, and to make it the basis of his own action—this is man's part. And so we may teach our children that the great and powerful God is not moving in their world in ways wholly past their finding out but that they may, through earnestly seeking to know and do his will, become in very truth co-workers with God.

When they see about them the vast stretches of barren desert, they may aspire to make it blossom as the rose. As they see the terrible ravages of disease, they may resolve to understand the causes and to overcome them. As they are surrounded by wars and conflict of group against group, nation against nation, race against race, they may dedicate themselves to good will and brotherhood. Thus will they be laying hold on the power of God by committing themselves to doing the will of God.

V

The Righteousness of God

IN A RAPID REVIEW OF THE OLD TESTAMENT ONE IS amazed to find how contemporary it is! A nation waxes great, assumes that it can conquer the earth, and meets disaster; a small nation seeks to escape destruction by making an alliance with a powerful one, and suffers disillusionment. A period of prosperity breeds love of wealth for its own sake, of lavish display of possessions, of overvaulting ambition, of inflated self-importance, of cruel oppression of the poor, and is followed by depression, revolution, national catastrophe. A people forget God, set up idols made of their own designing, concern themselves not with the things of God but solely with the things of men, despise the prophets who would recall them to God, spend their substance for that which satisfies not, and then find themselves in captivity in a strange land, suffering under oppression and cruel abuse.

The Judgment Upon Evil

Through the sweep of history, brought together into a few pages of narrative and comment, the Old Testament books recounting the story of men and of nations, age after age, set forth vividly and in long-time perspective the righteousness of God and his judgment upon evil. It is true that in some passages there is portrayal of the apparently capricious anger of God [1] and of his fierce denunciation of his people.[2] But the total picture is one of

[1] E.g., I Sam. 6:19; II Sam. 6:6-7.
[2] E.g., Isa. 10:5; Jer. 30:23.

49

righteousness vindicated rather than one of anger appeased. In the message of the great prophets "Thus saith the Lord" often served as the introduction to a pronouncement of disaster, but the disaster was the result of man's sin. "It was the unique characteristic of Jehovah that he was identified with the moral principle of the universe and that this principle was looked upon as absolutely sovereign." [3]

This conception was made clear in the words of Amos:

Thus saith Jehovah: For three transgressions of Israel, yea, for four, I will not turn away the punishment thereof; because they have sold the righteous for silver, and the needy for a pair of shoes; they that pant after the dust of the earth on the head of the poor, and turn aside the way of the meek.

They hate him that reproveth in the gate, and they abhor him that speaketh uprightly. Forasmuch therefore as ye trample upon the poor, and take exactions from him of wheat: ye have built houses of hewn stone, but ye shall not dwell in them; ye have planted pleasant vineyards, but ye shall not drink the wine thereof. For I know how manifold are your transgressions, and how mighty are your sins—ye that afflict the just, that take a bribe, and that turn aside the needy in the gate from their right.

Seek good, and not evil, that ye may live; and so Jehovah, the God of hosts, will be with you.

In the light of the history of man's life upon the earth it is surprising that he has not learned the truth so clearly revealed by these great prophets of Old Testament: man cannot reject the law of God, human beings cannot set themselves against the eternal moral order of the universe, without disaster. There are those who, looking upon the destruction and suffering over the earth today, are asking, "How can these things be if there is a God?"

[3] A. C. Knudson, *The Religious Teaching of the Old Testament*, Abingdon-Cokesbury, 1918, p. 155.

But as one great preacher put it, "Rather than asking, 'How can these things be if there is a God?' men should be confessing, '*Because* there is a God at work in the universe, disaster is come upon us as the consequence of our defiance of moral law.' "

The Reality of Moral Law

All this does not mean that God is seeking vengeance because man has refused to recognize his sovereignty, that he is measuring out suitable punishments and suffering for every sin of every man and of every nation in accordance with some vast system of bookkeeping. It does not mean that God sends wars, that he plans suffering for each transgression. Rather, such troubles are the inevitable result of violation of the moral law of the universe. There is evil in the world, terrible evil. It is necessary that judgment be passed upon evil in order that the moral structure of the universe be preserved. And the moral structure of the universe must be preserved if man is to have the opportunity to be man and not merely an animal or a robot. Conceivably, a world could have been created without moral law; but in such a world *man,* with unique capacity for freedom of choice, could not be. Without it, man could have no power of choice because there would be no basis of choice, no privilege of evaluating one experience above another because there would be no basis of value. "Woe unto them that call evil good, and good evil" is a statement of sober fact—a fact rooted in the nature of the universe rather than an arbitrary pronouncement.

In order to be granted the boon of freedom, man cannot be forced to choose the good. There must be allowed him the real opportunity to choose evil. And if he chooses evil he starts chains of events and situations which have

51

far-reaching consequences not only for himself but also for others whose lives touch his directly or indirectly. In this world of moral law, when greed, the struggle for prestige, the reaching after power, have loomed so large; when the prophets who would recall the nations to the righteousness of God go unheeded, then, in our own day as in all the other ages since man became man, disaster befalls. God may not abrogate the moral order of the universe without denying himself.

This is the sober truth which our children must be taught.

When Evil Seems to Triumph

What shall we say to our children when they ask us why the wicked prosper while the righteous suffer? This problem is as old as man. In our short view we cannot see the beginning or the end of the operation of moral law. Dr. Horton suggests that through history there is a grim process of action and reaction "in which the proud and cruel are usually victorious, and then meet Nemesis by overreaching themselves; and a quiet mysterious process of assimilation wherein the men of God win their way, against appalling obstacles, by soul-force alone." [4]

We may not tell our children that righteousness will always be triumphant. But we may invite them to share the faith of the Psalmist:

Fret not thyself because of evil-doers,
Neither be thou envious against them that work unrighteous-
ness. . . . .
Trust in the Lord, and do good; . . . .
Commit thy way unto the Lord; . . . .
Rest in the Lord, and wait patiently for him: . . . .
Depart from evil, and do good; . . . .

---

[4] W. M. Horton, *Realistic Theology*, Harper, 1934, p. 112.

For the Lord loveth justice,
And forsaketh not his saints.

In many specific situations in history the forces of evil do indeed appear to triumph, and righteousness appears to be overthrown. On the day of the Crucifixion the darkness that was over the face of the earth was more than physical darkness. It appeared to men that God himself had failed. But after that there came the Resurrection and Pentecost.

The Triumph of God's Righteousness

In challenging the people of their day to recognize the righteousness of God the great prophets made it clear that God would triumph, that his will would prevail, that ultimately righteousness would be established in the earth. Recognizing as they did the reality of man's sin and refusal to obey God, they came to accept the thought that God's rule might be delayed. By his rebellion man might delay it, because God had granted him the freedom to rebel; but no man or nation or combination of nations could prevent the final triumph of God's will in the earth.

In view of the extent of man's sin, some of the great prophets could not see how even God could bring about the universal acceptance of his purposes without first uprooting evil in some awful catastrophe. And so they prophesied that "doom surpassing anything known in the past was to befall Israel. War, captivity, fire, earthquake, eclipse, famine, pestilence—all these were used as symbols of the impending catastrophe. . . . . The Israel of history with its idolatry, its injustice, its immorality, its uncleanness of heart, would be swept away. . . . . Only righteousness and loyalty of soul would have a place in the new Israel that was to supersede the Israel of the past." [5]

[5] Knudson, *The Religious Teaching of the Old Testament,* pp. 167-68.

What shall we teach our children about the triumph of God in the world? Certainly the present condition of the world is not what God intended it to be. Into bold relief have been thrust the facts of injustice, cruelty, repression; hunger, cold, nakedness; over-vaulting ambition, greed, lust of power among the sons of men. Has God, then, turned from the world in utter denial? Will the righteous God of all the earth now rise in his power and visit destruction upon men and nations for their wickedness? There can be no doubt that current history has given impetus to the view that the Kingdom of God is to be established by catastrophic divine intervention, which will destroy the old world order and replace it with a new heaven and a new earth.

Neither can there be any doubt that current history has subdued the enthusiasm for the view held during recent years in many churches and very generally taught to children and youth, which describes the Kingdom of God in terms of a gradual establishment of human social and economic welfare largely through man's own efforts. In the presence of the destruction of so much of what has been called human progress—progress toward the goal of mutual aid and co-operation, toward the elimination of famine and pestilence and war and poverty—men have lost confidence in their own ability to "build" the Kingdom of God. Crashing down upon man's grandest achievements has come the most terrible devastation that has ever visited the planet, and that devastation has come from man's own hand. Is man, then, incapable of becoming a responsible worker in the Kingdom of God? Is the establishment of the Kingdom to be a consummation in which man has no part, an act of God shattering the pattern of history?

In view of the present confusion, it is well to review

the teachings of Jesus and to test our thinking by his, lest we allow ourselves to fall into error and teach our children false doctrine. Dean Weigle in his *Jesus and the Educational Method* suggests that it is in the light of Jesus' teaching about God that we must view his idea of the coming of God's kingdom, the triumph of his righteousness. From this point of view he describes three senses, related yet distinct, in which Jesus uses the phrase "Kingdom of God": as referring to the present rule of God in the universe; as referring to the sovereign will of God becoming effective in the lives of believers; and as referring to the final consummation in the earth of God's will.[6]

The *kingship* of God is not dependent upon the response of men. "God is King; men do not elect him." [7] His kingdom is an everlasting kingdom, and his dominion is from generation to generation, in the sense that God's sovereignty is eternal. It does not begin in a small way and grow because men support it. It *is*.

Yet the kingship of God is not merely cold reality. It is active in helping men. For Jesus made it clear in his teaching that God is not outside the world, withdrawn from it, observing it and judging but not participating in it. God is *in* the world, seeking to redeem men, all men of all races and all nations, to turn them from their evil ways. God is the righteous Judge, but the righteousness of God includes more than judgment upon men and nations. It includes a seeking after his children. The judgments of God are not primarily for punishment. They are primarily for redemption. By the terrible results of sin which catastrophe reveals, God is calling man

[6] L. A. Weigle, *Jesus and the Educational Method*, Abingdon-Cokesbury, 1939, p. 90.

[7] *Ibid.*, p. 78.

55

to fellowship with himself through responsive righteousness.

To respond to God, "to choose God rather than Satan or mammon or self as the ruler of his life, and to respond to God with faith, trust, obedience"—that is man's part. "As men thus accept and seek to fulfill God's will, the relation contemplated in his kingdom becomes effective on earth. It is a personal relation between God and human beings, both as individuals and as communities or people." [8] In the establishment of the Kingdom of God in this sense, the making effective in the lives of persons and nations of the will of God, man may rise to the full stature of sonship and be a responsible fellow worker with God, making a contribution to the realization of his purpose.

It seems clear that Jesus shared the view of the devout Jews of his day that the consummation of God's reign in the earth would come soon. But he thought of the consummation as ethical and universal rather than arbitrary and nationalistic. It was the faith of Jesus that the consummation of God's rule upon the earth will come in harmony with the character and the purposes of God. This is the goal toward which human history is directed. In this faith Jesus taught his disciples to pray, "Thy kingdom come. Thy will be done in earth, as it is in heaven." And it is in this faith that we may teach our children to pray today, not presuming that men will build this kingdom of themselves but recognizing it as the *response* of men to the love and the goodness, the righteousness and the mercy, the sovereignty and the kingship of God.

---

[8] *Ibid.*, p. 79.

VI

Children's Understanding of Jesus

A MONG THE FIRST STORIES TOLD TO LITTLE CHILDREN in Christian families are stories of Jesus. Many children come to think of him as a loving and beloved friend long before they think about his nature or his mission. Yet because parents and teachers are so eager to help their children to know and love Jesus, they sometimes speak of him in ways which introduce questions and problems before the child is ready to consider them.

How shall we introduce our children to Jesus? How shall we help them really to know him? How shall we interpret his life and work to them? How shall we lay sound foundations for a growing awareness of Jesus as the Son of God and a recognition of him as Savior?

Among the earnest and devout teachers of little children there are differences of opinion. There are some who feel that it is best to tell stories of Jesus as a good, kind man, just as we tell stories of other characters, with no attempt to set him apart as unique. They would include stories of other good men—Socrates, Paul, St. Francis, John Huss, William Penn—along with stories of Jesus, without differentiation. At the other extreme are those who would surround stories of Jesus, from the child's earliest experience, with the quality of luminous otherness, symbolized by the halo in all pictures used. They would stress the stories of the wondrous birth of Jesus, of the mysteries and the miracles in his life, rather that the evidences of his humanity.

There are real questions reflected here, questions of basic

importance for the religious development of children. Yet it seems clear that we need not set the points of view over against one another so directly as has sometimes been done.

Introducing the Little Child to Jesus

All that Jesus Christ is and means to men the little child may not comprehend. We shall not begin by attempting to explain doctrines about the person of Christ, the manner in which he is the Son of God. Rather, we shall begin at the "near end," at the point where the life of Jesus is most readily understood. We may begin with simple stories of Jesus as his life is recorded in the Gospels, of his kindness, of the way he helped people, of how he showed his love for others, especially, how he showed his love for children. These stories we may tell over and over, for little children enjoy the repetition of familiar stories, and we wish these stories to be known thoroughly.

What we shall attempt to give little children is an opportunity to form a clear picture of Jesus in his ministry of helpfulness and love. Then we may say to them, "Jesus loves us. God loves us as Jesus did. Jesus showed us what God is like."

As the children grow older we may select stories and sayings which show that Jesus knew the way of life which would enable persons to be truly happy. We may select stories which show respect for personality, regard for a person's own value, even though that person is unimportant or sick or an outcast. As we tell these stories we may say, "Jesus loves *all* people. Jesus knows what will make people happy. He shows us God's plan for his children to live together happily."

We shall not make the mistake of creating, by our selection, a picture of Jesus which lacks strength and courage. For growing boys and girls the selection of material from the life of Jesus must include stories which show Jesus standing fearlessly before powerful enemies; meeting on a plane of high skill and insight the "catch questions" of skillful lawyers; denouncing evil without hesitation or thought for his personal safety; demanding righteousness beyond that of the accepted code of the professional religious leaders of his day; facing physical torture without retreat.

Jesus should, then, be presented as a strong, friendly, lovable person so that little children may feel at home with him and so that growing boys and girls may feel drawn to him in admiration and devotion. But he should be so presented that children will early come to feel that, in some way which they do not fully comprehend, Jesus is unique among all the other good and brave men who ever lived. This feeling should rest upon the interpretation of the *character* and *personality* of Jesus, not upon miracles or upon ceremonies that have grown up around him. These matters are of little significance to little children; the *sort of person* Jesus was, is of great significance to them.

Teaching the Life of Jesus

By thus beginning with stories from the life of Jesus we may help little children to lay a sound foundation for understanding Jesus and responding to him. By the time they are seven or eight years of age children will be ready for a simple chronological story of the life of Jesus so that they may begin to see it in its wholeness. And we shall make every effort to be sure during the following years that they come really to know the story of Jesus as he lived among men. A large amount of confusion regarding the nature and mission of Jesus which later develops is due to lack of basic knowledge of the record of his life.

Without such knowledge, without an appreciation of

Jesus as a person among other persons—one who really lived in history, who shared the human nee. and joys and suffering of other persons—our children may not be expected to respond to interpretations of Jesus.

But merely to tell this story is not to give our children adequate help in understanding the significance of Jesus for their own lives and for the world. And so as they grow older there must be guidance in thinking of the nature and mission of Jesus. What may it mean to them when our children hear that Jesus revealed God to us, that he is the incarnate Son of God?

The Uniqueness of Jesus

Let us be careful not to set Jesus off from all other revelations of God as though he were unrelated to them. The writer to the Hebrews says, "God, having of old time spoken unto the fathers in the prophets by divers portions and in divers manners, hath at the end of these days spoken unto us in his Son." Thus he indicates that there is continuity between the revelation of God in the Old Testament and the revelation of God in Jesus. But whereas in speaking to men through the prophets God was limited by the nature of the prophets through whom he spoke, in speaking to men through Jesus he was speaking through one in whom sonship to God had been perfected.

It is clear that to the writers of the New Testament, Jesus was *other than* the great prophets or any contemporary rabbi or teacher. The writers report, with sympathy, his setting aside the Jewish law: "Ye have heard that it was said to them of old time, ... but I say unto you." This means that they accepted the personal word of Jesus as being above that of the established law. He could criticize it; he could say that it was to be superseded by a higher law. Again, they say of him, "He taught them as one having *authority*, and not as their scribes," setting him apart from the other teachers. Thus they acknowledged him as a prophet above the prophets, a teacher above the teachers, as one who could speak with authority for God. As Professor Moffatt puts it, "He taught and acted as one commissioned to make men decide for God, the King and Father whom he represented, and this meant that the decision for or against him determined human destiny." [1] He said with confident assurance, "Heaven and earth shall pass away, but my words shall not pass away." The law, the temple, the ceremonies of religion, will pass; but his revelation of God's will is to abide.

But Jesus did more than teach with authority. "He and his teachings were identified." He not only taught in the name of God; he actually was in his life the "Word of God" made manifest to man. Through Jesus, God was actually at work among men, manifesting to them his righteousness, his continuing love, his redeeming power. It was this "vision of God in Jesus Christ" which supplied the impulse of life and hope in the early Christians, whose writings became the New Testament. The faith which this vision inspires is the faith by which vast numbers of humble men of all races have lived, and it is the faith which we may help our children realize for themselves.

The Miracles in Their Setting

If this be our approach to interpreting the nature of Jesus to our children, there will not likely be any serious problems with respect to the stories of the wondrous birth and the miracles. In the first place, stories of wonders rarely arouse questions in the thoughts of children. But, more important, the *life* of Jesus—his graciousness, his concern

---

[1] James Moffatt, *Jesus Christ the Same,* Abingdon-Cokesbury, 1940, p. 95.

for others, his forgiveness of enemies—his life itself is, to those who consider it thoughtfully, more wonder-inspiring than incidents which we have come to call miracles.

We may, then, tell our children the beautiful stories of the birth of Jesus for the joy they will bring—not to *prove* to children that Jesus was the Son of God. In the telling we may give ourselves and our children opportunity to pause in joyous wonder while we hear the angels' song and see the guiding star. But it will be upon the *simplicity* of the earthly environment of the baby Jesus that we will dwell, for we wish our children to love this baby.

Few children will raise questions regarding the manner in which the life of Jesus began. And few parents or teachers will wish to raise any such questions with children. If children do raise questions we shall try to answer them simply, in accordance with our best knowledge and most sincere belief. God is the Lord of life, and there is no doubt that there are areas of creative power quite beyond human understanding. But for most Christians the evidences in the life and work of Jesus are more moving and more challenging to faith in his unique nature and mission than is the manner of his entrance into life. We shall, then, not introduce little children to problems which are beyond their understanding. Rather, we shall encourage them to share our wonder in the thought that the God of all the earth chose to send a little baby to grow up in a humble family and be a friend and helper to all men as the very best way to show men what God is like. He might have sent a king in royal splendor; he might have sent an army of angels. But, instead, he sent a baby to live in the home of a village carpenter.

Regarding the miracles recorded as part of the earthly life of Jesus, let it be remembered that miracles are happenings which men do not understand. Perhaps as we

62

grow in understanding of Jesus, we may grow also in understanding of all his acts. But as we grow in understanding of Jesus, it will be Jesus himself, his purposes, his mission, his whole personality, which will become increasingly important to us. His deeds were not a series of unrelated, spectacular feats. They were part of a pattern of life which reflects in every part his basic purpose. Men were suffering; he relieved them. Men were hungry; he fed them. Men were frightened; he comforted them. Men were penitent; he forgave them. Men were yearning for God; he showed them the Father.

Just *how* he ministered to those who needed him, we do not know. And it need not trouble us. Again let it be said that the life of Jesus does not require the support of miracles to prove that it was a life of special, unique quality. One who seeks to enter into the spirit of Jesus finds infinitely more wonder in the thought of his praying as he hangs in agony upon the cross, "Father, forgive them; for they know not what they do," than he finds in the story of his feeding a multitude from the food in a boy's lunch.

And so we shall tell the stories of the deeds of Jesus simply, reverently, without either stressing or "sliding over" the fact that some things which he did are beyond our understanding but relating always what he did to the purpose which lay back of it. If our children ask questions about how he healed sick people, we shall hear them quietly and answer them to the best of our own understanding. But we shall answer them humbly, not dogmatically, leaving to the child the right to his own thoughts after we have shared our own with him. The important matter is not whether the child finds it satisfying to think that actual, physical miracles took place or whether he finds it more satisfying to believe that it is human ignorance which shrouds these happenings but which someday will give way to understanding. The important result is the response of the child to the total personality of Jesus.

Jesus as the Great Example

This response will, we hope, include the desire to live in accordance with the example of Jesus. This does not mean that one's life will be in detail like his life. He lived under different social, geographical, and economic conditions. To copy his dress, his food, his mode of travel—this is not suggested. Rather, to follow him, to be loyal to him, to build one's life on the conviction that his interpretation of life and of human relationships was the eternally right and good interpretation—this is what is suggested. To assume that Jesus may, in matters of human conduct and attitude, be a pattern for men is not out of harmony with the view that Jesus is also Lord and Savior.

The writer of Hebrews, as Professor Moffatt points out, after portraying the unique sacrifice of Jesus for sin and his supreme position in heaven, also presents him as a pattern for men. He calls upon men to look to Jesus as the "pioneer and the perfection of faith" if they would be true to the heroic course in their own lives. He gave a "living example of human faithfulness to God when he met and mastered such trials as shame and pain." [2]

The will of God for human life is revealed in the life of Jesus. His way of living with his fellow men, not as one who pleased himself, but as one who gave first thought to the good of others; his standard of values, which emphasized, not prestige or power or wealth, but simple kindness and steadfast loyalty to the right; his primary purpose in life, which was not to realize his own ambitions but to do the will of God—in these experiences Jesus showed us the high purpose for man which is in the heart of God.

[2] *Jesus Christ the Same*, p. 100.

64

Because there are in the recorded life of Jesus incidents which tell in direct and appealing fashion of the way Jesus lived, we may give our children direct guidance in the way of life which is the *good way* for them and for all men. There will have to be, of course, some interpretation in terms of present-day child-life situations. Jesus did not live in an industrialized, mechanized civilization as our children do. Some situations which they must face are not pictured in the Gospels. But they can find there ways of relating themselves to other persons and ways of relating themselves to God and his purposes which are basic to any particular situation.

When Jesus was faced with tremendous personal decisions, he went away into a quiet place and prayed—not for a few hurried moments, but sometimes for the whole night. The decisions which we and our children face are not identical with those he faced, but we also face personal decisions of importance. Do we imitate Jesus at such moments? When Jesus was offered "the kingdom of the earth" to betray the will of God, he turned his back upon the temptation. Do we imitate him when we have opportunities to promote personal advantage at the cost of betraying loyalty to the *best* we know?

When Jesus was seeking rest in the house of a friend after a very busy and difficult day, the sick and the lonely and the distressed were brought to him; and he ministered to them long after a normal "working day" was ended. Do we imitate him in concern for the unattended sick and the lonely and distressed persons in our community even when it interferes with our comfort and convenience? When Jesus was surrounded by crowds of people listening to his words and they brought little children to him, he turned from the crowd to the children and gave them his loving friendship. Do we imitate him in our readiness to give ourselves in happy, unselfish friendship to the "unimportant" persons about us, even when it means foregoing some "important" social opportunity?

When Jesus saw corruption and greed flourishing in the Temple market, he denounced the offenders fearlessly though he knew it would bring him into crucial conflict with powerful leaders in the community. Do we imitate him in courageously standing for justice and honesty in all the institutions of our community? When Jesus was weary from the strain of crowds of people and discouraging happenings, he sought refreshment and strength in communion with God. Do we imitate him when we feel in need of refreshment after hard work and frustrating situations?

Yes, we may teach our children that in the life of Jesus they can find revealed the way of life which they may follow with assurance that it is the way which will bring them happiness and make their lives useful and inspiring to their fellows. We may help them to see how in everyday situations and relationships they can be followers of Jesus.

But there must be a caution: unless there is an ever-increasing appreciation of the total personality of Jesus, there is not likely to be either the desire or the ability on the part of children to imitate him in specific situations. To tell isolated stories from the life of Jesus for the purpose of "pointing a moral" is not a helpful way to interpret him to boys and girls as their great example. It must be said again that it is important for the boys and girls to have a thorough knowledge of the life of Jesus so that they may respond to him as a *person* first of all. Then they will be eager to know in more detail just what he taught about the good way to live and will feel moved to follow that way for themselves.

The Crucifixion

With all its goodness and beauty, the life of Jesus ended

in the most ignominious death that could be inflicted upon a man in his day. He was condemned to be executed, publicly, by crucifixion. How can we interpret this fact to boys and girls?

Of course we shall not tell the little children about the crucifixion of Jesus. They must know of his *life* before they know of his death. But after they go to school we could not keep it from them if we would; so we must be prepared to interpret it to them.

The basis of our interpretation may be the fact that people suffer for being good as well as for being bad. As has already been suggested, it is likely that children will early have experience of suffering for their convictions if their convictions run counter to the established customs of the community. A child who insists upon fairness to a child of a minority race may find himself, also, excluded from the games or the parties. And so the thought that good men suffer for their very goodness in a world that is not good may be understood as soon as the child has come into contact with such situations.

If our presentation of the life of Jesus has shown him strongly resisting evil, standing against the rulers of his nation and of his church because they insisted upon a narrow, unloving thought of God and of human relations, they will know that he is not going to have an easy life. He was threatening the prestige of the learned ones because he was setting aside their teachings; he was threatening the established order in the church because he was insisting that honesty and kindness were more important than the observance of established ceremonies; he was threatening the incomes of influential leaders because he insisted upon overthrowing customs which were impoverishing the poor and enriching the rich. He was in conflict with these powerful forces for the very reason that he was *good*. And so they sought to do away with him.

But Jesus was more than a social reformer; he was the revelation of the will of God to men. He knew himself to be sent by God to proclaim his will among men. Thus he spoke with authority for God. And this fact, the fact that he dared to speak in the name of God, made his life and work especially disturbing to the men of his day. They did not want to hear the will of God thus proclaimed; they did not want to acknowledge their sins; they did not want to recognize Jesus as the one sent of God to save men from their sins by winning them to loyalty to God.

Jesus knew that his mission was leading him to his death. He could have escaped the Cross if he had compromised. But to him, to do the will of God was the supreme good, and so he did not falter.

Jesus did not deliberately choose his own death, he accepted it as a divine appointment, as a part of his mission. He was sent into the world to establish the kingdom of God, the ideal state both of righteousness and of human welfare; and in sacrificing his life for his ideal he revealed in a supreme way both his love for mankind and his personal holiness. And not only did he reveal his own righteousness and love, he revealed the righteousness and love of God. For God was in Christ reconciling the world to himself. What Christ did in his supreme act of self-sacrifice, that God did. It was in this way that the love and righteousness of God were proclaimed by the death of Christ. The event itself was a mirror of the heart of God.[3]

As our boys and girls grow older they will consider the formulation by their church of doctrines about the death of Jesus. But while they are children the simplest and the

[3] A. C. Knudson, *The Doctrine of Redemption*, Abingdon-Cokesbury, 1933, p. 377.

most direct interpretation will lay the soundest foundation for growing understanding.

It should go without saying that we shall not harrow boys and girls with detailed descriptions of the actual crucifixion proceedings. Rather, we should help them to understand why Jesus was able to face the shame and suffering with courage and faith in the goodness of God.

And we should be very careful not to let the story end with the crucifixion. That was *not* the end.

"Alive For Evermore"

How may we help our children to think of Jesus, not only as a person who lived in Palestine long ago, but as one who is "alive for evermore"? In what sense may we interpret to our children the thought that Jesus not only showed them what is right but is now helping them to do it? Little children often do not need any "interpretation" to enable them to feel that someone whom they do not see is near them. They often engage in conversation with faraway grandmothers and imaginary playmates in a very realistic fashion. There are many reports from mothers of conversations which their children hold with Jesus in this same spirit. But we are thinking of something other than this type of experience.

A person may be deeply aware of fellowship with someone who is physically absent, not in the make-believe sense of the little child's games with imaginary playmates, nor in the sense of vivid dreaming, but in the sense of real communion of spirits. Without overemphasizing the experience, we may lift it up and suggest that among persons who really love one another there often is a feeling of togetherness even when they are far apart. When his mother is away, for instance, a child who loves her and trusts her feels oftentimes that she is really near by, helping

69

him to remember to "be good." We may feel that Jesus goes on loving all children today, just as he loved children when he was watching them playing games in the market place of Capernaum, and that he goes on helping them, too. When they think of him and of what he did or of what he said, they feel near to him and are grateful for his love.

There is no doubt from the Gospel record that the disciples were vividly aware of Jesus after his death. They were altogether sure that he had triumphed over death and was "alive for evermore." After the awful days of the arrest, trial, and crucifixion of their Master, there came upon the disciples a terrible fear and sense of utter defeat. They hid themselves away from men. Their hopes were dead; life had no meaning; they saw no future. Then they learned that Jesus was not dead; he was alive. And they were amazingly transformed. They boldly proclaimed a message that astonished their listeners. They spoke with such courage and insight and conviction that even unfriendly judges were amazed and dared not restrain them.

For the early disciples the belief in the Resurrection was no mere doctrine; it was life itself. It made all the difference between despair and confidence, between failure and triumph. If we tell the story of the life of Jesus to our children and end it with the cross, we are not telling all the story. For it is a truth attested by the experience of men and women through hundreds of years and in all nations that his life has gone on, encouraging the despairing, strengthening the weak, bringing joy to the sorrowful, companionship to the lonely, comfort to the suffering, steadfastness to the tempted.

We shall be equally unwise, however, if the story of the Resurrection is emphasized to the neglect of simpler phases of the life of Jesus. It is a beautiful, vivid, and moving story; but if told without proper background of a real ac-

70

quaintance with the life of Jesus, it may easily become, not a source of joy and comfort, but a source of confusion and fear. It is the life which lay before it which gives it power. Detached from the life of Jesus, or told against a background of vague understanding of his life and work, it is a wonder story; told as a part of his life of righteousness and love and service, it is the glorious and inevitable climax of the whole. For a life such as his *could not* be ended when his body was broken by sinful men. His life had expressed abiding values, deathless love. And so we may teach our children that Jesus lives today, not because of some isolated, wonder-inspiring event, but because there was in his life that quality, that spirit, which is of the very essence of eternity.

"Ye Shall Live Also"

"Because I live, ye shall live also." Because Jesus touched human life and lifted it up so that it could realize its full possibilities, because he showed men how they could achieve the destiny God intended for them as children of the Father, he opened wide to them the gates of eternal life.

Children often ask questions about the future life, and these questions require thoughtful consideration. It is only in the light of the life and teachings of Jesus that we may answer them confidently. When the Sadducees came to him with questions about the future life he answered them in terms of the character of God. His faith in eternal life was rooted in his faith in God. As has already been pointed out, Jesus gave us no ground for an interpretation of God's love in terms of material prosperity and freedom from struggle. He specifically renounced for himself any expectation of special privilege. His thought of God was not bound down by material concern. And so we do not find his thoughts of eternal life dwelling upon material rewards. He left us no blueprint of heaven, no catalogue of its beauties and comforts.

Neither does Jesus speak of the future life as if it were wholly disconnected with the present. Throughout his teaching he spoke of the kingship of God as eternal. It is real in the present as in the future, in earth as in heaven. The goal he puts before men is the attaining of fullness of life by entering the Kingdom in the present, not only looking forward to it in a distant future. That there is a future he is sure, but there is also a present which is related to that future. In the future life temporary, individual concerns are brought into broader perspective. It will be life not bound down by the limitations of the flesh but free and glorious, life not limited by time and space but eternal and boundless. Death marks a transition in life within the Kingdom, not an end of one life and the beginning of another altogether different.

Jesus' thought of eternal life, then, is reflected in his thought of present life lived in obedience to the will of God and in consciousness of the love of God. Jesus clearly taught that God's care includes concern for the material needs of his children. To many persons the struggle for bread to keep themselves and their children alive is a bitter reality. To all such persons, as well as to us who have never known cruel want, Jesus says, "Your Father knoweth that ye have need of these things." It seems clearly to be the thought of Jesus that all men who trust their lives to God may confidently expect in the future that *life* will be granted—life not threatened by desperate struggle to sustain it but life fully and abundantly assured by the purpose and the gift of God.

Jesus also taught that in the present world those who seek to do the will of God will be freed from stress and tension and anxiety. He taught that for those who com-

72

mit their ways unto God all effort may be directed toward getting useful work done, with no energy consumed in worry and fretfulness and resentment. He taught that suffering may be creative and not futile. In Jesus' thought, this freedom from tension, wasteful effort, futile suffering, which may be realized but imperfectly in this present life, will be fully experienced in the life to come. In peace and serenity persons will be able to devote themselves wholly and joyously to sharing in the great purposes of God.

Again, Jesus offered to those who seek membership in the Kingdom of God the expectation that their sense of fellowship with others will be enlarged, the strain of competition overcome, and that in place of rivalry there will come an ever-widening and deepening experience of brotherhood. Hate and suspician will diminish because man's thoughts will be centered, not upon his own advancement, power, and prestige, but upon the welfare of the family of God. The ties that bind his life to others in satisfying love and service will thus be multiplied and made stronger.

This enlargement and enrichment of one's relationships with one's fellows, begun in the present life, will be carried to perfection in the life to come. In the future life *all* barriers which separate men from their fellows will be done away—barriers between family and family, between race and race, between nation and nation, between class and class, between ages gone by and ages to come—all will be done away. In complete understanding and sympathy the noble souls of all ages, nations, races, will be able to engage joyously in co-operative activities, sharing the common purpose of doing the will of God.

Finally, to men who trust themselves to God, Jesus promised fellowship with the Father. To Jesus this was the supreme good of life, that for which all else might well be lost. But earth-bound creatures, subject to the limitations of the flesh, cannot enter fully into fellowship with God; they cannot fully apprehend the kingship of God nor the fatherhood of God. In the thought of Jesus, the earthly life is but the beginning of the heavenly life which will follow, when men may see life more nearly as God sees it, when things are viewed no longer from the narrow perspective of our personally centered experiences but rather "in the light of eternity." In this glorious life of the future men will know God, will understand his purposes, will experience fully his fellowship. "And this is life eternal, that they should know thee the only true God, and him whom thou didst send, even Jesus Christ."

Is the expectation of life in the heavenly home a selfish expectation, suggesting a seeking for reward? Of course, concentration upon future blessedness to the disregard of present opportunities and obligations is dangerous. But as we have seen, in the thought of Jesus there is no such separation between the present and the future life in the Kingdom of God. Only those who live to the full the present life that is vouchsafed them can be ready to enter the future life that is immeasurably extended. Such a thought of the future life, far from distracting one, adds greatly to one's participation in the present work of the world while at the same time it releases one from bondage to the present.

Is such a thought of eternal life one which we can share confidently with our children? Rather than attempting to describe heaven, can we share with them our expectation that the future life will afford companionship with the great souls of all the ages? Instead of centering attention upon release from effort, can we help them to look forward to release from strains caused by jealousies and bad tempers and selfishness, so that they can always be their very best selves? Instead of speaking of material comforts, can we lead them to think of the joy of knowing the answers to so many puzzling questions of life, of really understanding? Instead of arousing hopes of power and prestige, can we guide them into appreciation of the happiness of fellowship with God that is uninterrupted by our carelessness and our sin?

To fail to offer our children guidance in thinking of the future life is to fail as Christian teachers. To attempt to go beyond such guidance is to attempt to do more than teachers may do. Just what heaven is like, no living man can know. But Jesus has shown us that God is love. To God, Jesus trusted his future life in complete confidence. And in this may we not follow him?

VII

Children and Salvation

NOT MANY YEARS AGO THERE WAS HIGH EXPECTATION that war and poverty and famine and disease would be banished from the earth by man's efforts, that through his inventions and his economics and his social progress the ills that have beset the race would be overcome. There was also the expectation that individual persons, through specialized methods of education, could overcome maladjustments that caused them to be unfriendly, cruel, selfish, and could become co-operative, useful, and happy persons. That is, there was high hope that man in the strength of his own power could rise to ever nobler heights of social and individual achievement.

This confidence in man is in many respects both noble and useful. The contrasting doctrine of the utter depravity and helplessness of man offers little incentive to high endeavor. If man is to make progress toward ideals, he must have confidence that he has the capacity to grow and that his efforts are important. He must have a sense of responsibility for being the noblest person he can be, for doing all that he can do to improve society. Moreover, he must work without ceasing to learn all he can learn about ways in which he can help other human personalities: through understanding their bodies so diet and exercise may be prescribed to make them sturdy; through understanding their minds and emotions so plans may be made to avoid difficulties and keep them healthful; through understanding their aspirations so guidance may be afforded toward wholesome fulfillment.

Man's Need of God

However, though man needs to have confidence in his ability to grow and to make a contribution to the welfare of the human family, his sense of self-sufficiency has led to serious consequences. His efforts in his own strength to save himself and to save society have failed. They have revealed to him his dire need of wisdom and insight and goodness far beyond his own powers. "Wretched man that I am! who shall deliver me out of the body of this death?" —the cry of Paul finds an echo in the hearts of thoughtful persons of this age who have struggled in vain to achieve for themselves and for others release from evil tendencies and escape from the consequences of their failures. At long last they realize that the love of God is the only ground of confidence in individual salvation and in the salvation of society, of which they are a responsible part.

This recognition of dependence upon God has, among some groups, brought a swingback to a view of man and of God which affirms that man is "nothing" and that God is "all in all." "Salvation is of the Lord" is interpreted to mean that man can merely wait upon God's good pleasure. Man's sin can be removed, but the initiative is wholly in the hands of God; and if society is to be saved at all, it will be only by direct act of God, which man may view as an onlooker, not as a participant.

What shall be our attitude toward the matter of sin and salvation in teaching children? How shall we help our children to be in very truth "children of God"?

Why Do Men Sin?

Clearly our emphasis will not be upon stirring up in our children a vague, depressing "sense of sin." In little children, as in all human personalities, there are capacities for

77

goodness and capacities for evil: tendencies toward co-operation, affection, and the desire to help others; and tendencies toward selfishness, toward using situations to their own advantage, toward neglecting the needs and interests of others. We must not be sentimentalists about our children: we must know them, as we know ourselves, to be persons within whom there is conflict between the good and the evil, and we must know that there is nothing simple and easy about the matter of its resolution. We shall try to help our children to recognize in themselves those quite specific attitudes, thoughts, and deeds toward God, toward other persons, and toward their own best selves, which fall short of the highest of which they are capable; and we shall help them to know that they are responsible to God for these failures.

We shall recognize and help our children to recognize that sin is the result, on the one hand, of man's freedom to choose and to evaluate for himself; and, on the other, of the difficulties of making choices in harmony with the requirements of God's will as expressed in moral law. As has already been said, if man is to have freedom of choice, it must be possible for him to choose evil. The *possibility* of sin, therefore, is readily understood. But it is not so easy to understand why the *actuality* of sin is universal among men. Why does man not avoid sin?

Let us be clear, in the first place, that the will of God presents high demands. Because it is the will of God, it is perfect goodness. To bring all the tendencies and impulses with which a human being is endowed to this level is necessarily enormously difficult.

In view of the fact that we begin life on the nonmoral plane, that there are within us numerous conflicting impulses and desires, that the moral sense dawns and develops only slowly, and that the task of transforming the natural into the spiritual is one that requires for its perfect fulfillment ceaseless vigilance throughout life, it is not strange nor is it out of harmony with human freedom that all men should have sinned. Indeed, the exceeding strange thing would be that anyone should live for any length of time in the world without sinning. The psychological and social forces that militate against obedience to the moral law are so numerous and so insistent that yielding to them at some time or other would seem almost inevitable.[1]

Again, man lives in the midst of a society in which all about him are occasions of stumbling. There are incentives to self-interest, offers of reward for achievement even at the cost of injustice to others, standards of success which ignore the will of God. Customs of group life, habits and institutions within a community, often have evil embedded in them so deeply that one is almost certainly involved in it by the very act of being a part of the community.

If the question be raised, "Why should a good God have made the conditions of attaining moral perfection so difficult?" there will be differing answers. No one may presume to give the final answer. It is, however, significant that those who have fought the good fight most strenuously seldom complain of the difficulty of the struggle.

Children and the Gospel[2]

In teaching children, the tendency has been to direct thought toward positive goodness rather than toward failures to achieve it. And it will be agreed that positive goodness should be emphasized in our program for children.

---

[1] Knudson, *The Doctrine of Redemption*, p. 265.

[2] In this section the author has drawn upon the pamphlet *The Evangelism of Children*, prepared by her for the International Council of Religious Education.

But there is a place also, as children learn to make their own choices, for helping them to recognize the reality of evil and the consequences which attend it. We must not expect too much of children, but neither must we expect too little of them. In their own experience they can understand how careless disregard of the needs and rights of others brings about suffering and sorrow; how selfishness brings about a lack of sympathy and fellowship with one's associates; how failure to do the best one knows brings about unhappiness within one's own inner self; how careless disregard of God's purposes as one has come to understand them brings about a sense of separateness from God. They can see the results in disease, misery, and squalor of the social sins within a community which deprives large numbers of its citizens of the opportunity for health and happiness. As they grow older they can begin to understand the terrible consequences in world-wide catastrophe of sin among men and nations.

Boys and girls are aware of tendencies to sin in their own lives. They know what Paul was talking about when he said, "The good which I would I do not: but the evil which I would not, that I practise." They ask many questions: "Why do I so often forget when I really do want to do right?" "Why do I lose my temper when I really do want to be friendly?" How may we help our children to come to understand God's plan of salvation for themselves and for all men? How may we be evangelists to our children?

Dr. Visser 't Hooft suggests that evangelism is "confronting" men with the Gospel. How does one confront children with the Gospel? As has already been pointed out, the child's approach to God is often through human fellowship. In confronting him with the Gospel, we may begin by confronting him with persons who believe the Gospel. The child whose home life is truly Christian has the greatest help that can come to him. In such a home the Gospel is made manifest through daily experience. Parents can let their children know that they seek insight and comfort and forgiveness from God and that they receive them. They can let their children know that, though "the sin which doth so easily beset" men is very real, the love of God makes it possible for them to overcome sin.

In the fellowship of the Christian Church, too, children may be confronted with the Gospel. Here they will be associated with persons who act upon the faith that God's grace can enable men to rise to heights formerly undreamed of, in generous self-giving, in preferring one another, in helping the weak. And beyond this present living fellowship is the compassing about of the noble souls of the ages who had faith in God's redeeming love. By providing opportunity for our children to become acquainted with the lives and aspirations and convictions of the men and women of the past and of the present to whom God has been the supreme reality, the source of insight and wisdom, of comfort and courage, we may help the children to enrich their own experience and to venture out to nobler faith.

It is supremely in the life of Jesus that we may confront our children with the Gospel. The good news which Jesus brought, the good news of God's love, of man's worth as a child and a creature of God, taught men that they could depend upon this seeking love of God to redeem them from sin. In his mission "to seek and to save that which was lost," Jesus showed us that no change in God's nature or purpose was necessary for man's salvation: God has always been, is now, and ever shall be the forgiving Father, eagerly desiring his son's return from the "far country" of his self-centeredness; the tender shepherd, seeking in the rough places of the earth for the sheep which have become lost.

81

Not even when man denies God, does the divine love falter. On the cross Jesus prayed, "Father, forgive them," revealing the greatness of the love of God for his children while they are yet sinners. In the Cross there is given us, at once, the perfect revelation of God's love and the perfect example of man's devotion to the will of God.

Jesus believed that through him God was effecting a mighty action for the salvation of men. This does not mean that he felt himself to be wringing it from the hand of God. . . . . It was God's initiative, God's action. His part was to obey, to be used of God, to do his Father's will, and so to reveal that will to men and lead them too to receive and accept it.[3]

Thus, if we are to confront children with the Gospel, we must confront them with Jesus Christ, who in his life and in his death made the Gospel known to men. As they are thus made aware of the love of God and of the nobility of a life which responds without reserve to this love, they will become aware of their own sins and shortcomings. As they become increasingly aware of the Good News which Jesus brought, they will become increasingly aware of their need for salvation, which only the acceptance of this Gospel for themselves will make possible. It is the sunlight which reveals the hidden dust of a long-unused room; so it is the light of the Gospel which reveals to men how far they have fallen short of their high calling as children of God.

Too often the emphasis upon salvation has been solely negative: salvation *from* sin. It must be also positive: salvation *for* useful and joyous living. "I came that they may have life, and may have it abundantly!" Jesus said. In release from the hampering sins which so easily beset him and in positive rejoicing in life which he knows to be

---

[3] Weigle, *Jesus and the Educational Method*, p. 100.

good, man finds the happiness which in other ways he has sought in vain. A modern teacher renders the words: "I came that they might have life, and *live it to the full!*"

This interpretation of salvation we must bring to our children. It brings a new, positive outlook, and life takes on fresh meaning and significance. There is release from strain and worry, resulting from the struggle for prestige and success, because when one has entrusted his life to God, these matters seem unimportant. There are opportunities for enlarged fellowship with one's fellows because barriers will have been done away when one acknowledges all men as one's brothers. One may have life and may *live it to the full!*

The Response to the Gospel

But since man is man, and not a robot, he must *accept* the salvation which is offered. God is able to save men from their sins; he is following them with seeking, redemptive love; but so long as man refuses to respond to this love, his salvation is delayed. Children can early be led to understand that there are some things which those who love them cannot do for them. No matter how much parents and teachers may wish to help their children, they are dependent upon the co-operation of the children themselves. Parents cannot make children strong unless the children accept the good food that is provided. They cannot make them have happy times with their playmates unless the children themselves accept the conditions of having happy times. Devoted parents and the most skillful teachers cannot give a child an education unless the child himself accepts the opportunities to learn.

So, as they grow, children can come to understand that God does not *make* his children commit their ways unto him. He helps them, and they can avail themselves of his help to the extent that they desire his help. The child's part is, thus, to recognize his need of God, to accept the help of God, to respond to the love of God with answering love and trust and devotion to his will.

The Part of the Teacher

Does the teacher or pastor or parent have an important part in the evangelism of boys and girls? Certainly no teacher can "save" a child! That is the work of God. Dean Weigle suggests the analogy of the work of a physician.

No physician ever heals a patient. All that the physician can do is to clear the way for natural forces to function properly. He can remove obstructions and disturbing factors, clean up infections, bind wounds, set broken bones, cut out malignant tissue, plan a regimen of food, air, exercise, and rest which will bring re-enforcement at points where it is most needed—but nature does the healing. Like growth, healing comes from God. So too no teacher ever creates insight or will or character; no evangelist ever saves a soul.[4]

The parent or teacher or pastor who would be a co-worker with God in the nurture of children, will accept a large measure of responsibility for removing stumbling blocks which keep the child from drawing near to God, for clearing away hindrances which are rooted in the environment of the child, for sharing with the child his own experiences and his own best insights into the purposes of God, for helping the child to understand the language in which God speaks to him.

In all this we are not suggesting that teachers speak to children directly of "the plan of salvation." Such a phrase is beyond their comprehension. And outlines, dia-

---

[4] *Jesus and the Educational Method*, p. 120.

84

grams, and "steps," they cannot follow. Moreover, it must always be borne in mind that no teacher may presume to tell children just how God will save them. We do not know. Sometimes it seems as if a person wakes up suddenly and thinks to himself: Why, now I am free from the old bad habits and evil thoughts and selfish desires! Now I can do the good things that I would do. Sometimes persons seem to learn little by little, year by year, as they grow. We may not lay down a pattern for God's action nor for our children's response to God.

It was Jesus who said, "Except ye turn, and become as little children, ye shall in no wise enter into the kingdom of heaven." Adults who have become self-sufficient, proud, find it hard to commit their way unto the Lord and trust in him. They have built up their own standards, their own plans, and set their own direction and goals. They must be halted, turned around. And only as they recognize, in the spirit of a child, their dependence upon God and entrust the direction of their lives to him, may they be saved.

But children *are* children! They do not have to become as children. The sense of dependence, of willingness to recognize their need of direction is alive in them. They have not charted their own course from which they must be recalled. Why, then, do we not give more attention to the matter of helping children while they are children to acknowledge their dependence upon God and to ask for his help in setting the course of their lives, to be ready to follow that course joyously, wholeheartedly?

Following the Law of Growth

Such approaches the teacher will make with careful attention to the experiences and capacities of the growing boys and girls. He will seek to understand children, how

85

they learn, how they respond to situations. He will call upon the best resources available in the field of child psychology and education. He will recognize that bad workmanship in this field, as in all others, hinders progress toward a goal and that in this field it is far more serious than in any other because larger values are at stake. He will not assume that good intentions are enough. He will study to show himself approved before God, a workman that does not need to be ashamed.

Through fellowship with Christians in their homes, in their churches, and in their communities; through fellowship with the great souls of the ages whose experiences are recorded in the Bible and in great religious literature; and supremely, through fellowship with God himself made manifest in Jesus Christ, growing boys and girls may be confronted with the Gospel. But always it must be remembered that children do not "learn" something and then "apply" it. They learn it, primarily, through experiencing it.

Teachers and pastors will know that they must not expect of little children the understanding and the consistent devotion which they may expect of adults. In dealing with children there will be the expectation that God's law of growth will apply in this realm as in all others. But while they are children they may know that their lives are in God's keeping. With the help of their more mature friends in the home and in the church, children may grow in understanding of the meaning of salvation and in the recognition of God's will for their lives; they may come increasingly to know what it offers them and what it requires of them.

The Significance of Commitment

There will come a time when parents and teachers and

pastors will help boys and girls to bring to focus their experiences, their aspirations, their sense of repentance, their apprehension of the gospel, and to give definite expression to their purpose to live in its light. There will come a time when there should be definite explication of the Christian faith on the part of parents, teachers, and pastors, and a definite commitment to it on the part of boys and girls. There should be sharpened up for them the necessity of making a real choice for the direction of their lives; they should be helped to become aware of "the challenge of God," of the necessity of making a decision between the will of God and their own will. In this choice lies their glorious opportunity to realize their possibilities as children of God. When the choice is made, when they allow the spirit of Christ to take the direction of their lives, then they may know that they have taken their place as children who share their Father's purposes as responsible co-operating members of his family.

The exact age at which such commitment should be expected and the form it should take will depend upon the experiences of the child, his home influences, the customs of his particular communion, and the attitude of the local church teachers and pastor. Whether there should be a public expression of the commitment before the congregation, or whether it should remain a quiet, personal experience; whether it should be related to the assumption of the vows of full membership in the church, or whether it should be regarded as a separate experience— such questions as these must be considered by the child with his parents and teachers. It is not likely that in the life of any person there will be a "final" commitment in the sense that no further act of dedication will ever be required. Most mature Christians have found that there are, throughout life, recurring occasions of repentance and commitment when new problems arise or new insights are gained. But there may be, and frequently is, one experience which sets the direction of all one's life purposes. It is of first importance, therefore, that all children be definitely aware of occasions of conscious commitment of their lives to the will of God on the level of their own experience.

The teachers, parents, and pastors of boys and girls have the opportunity of co-operating with God in interpreting to them the divine plan of salvation and in helping them to accept it in their lives. They can help them to understand the gospel that Jesus brought into the world, the good news that God loves men, that he will help every child to overcome those tendencies to self-seeking which lead to suffering and unhappiness, those desires for personal advantage which lead to frustration and disaster, that God will help him to be free to live a life of joyous fellowship with the Eternal. They can help them to make a choice to devote themselves to the will of God rather than to their own will, to *accept* the salvation which God freely offers.

VIII

Learning to Do God's Will

"WHY CALL YE ME, LORD, LORD, AND DO NOT THE things which I say"? was asked long ago of those who wished to enjoy the privileges of fellowship with their Master but who were reluctant to make their own the way of life which he taught. The same question is being asked today.

How shall we answer it for ourselves and teach our children to answer it? It is clear that countless men and women and boys and girls who have been moved by love of God to repent of their sins and to accept the plan of salvation which he offers, have yet failed miserably when it has come to realizing their expressed purpose to live their lives in devotion to the will of God.

Is it perhaps that we have been mistaken in expecting more of ourselves? Is it that we have assumed man to be capable of understanding the purposes of God and of sharing them, while, in reality, the absolute "otherness" of God makes this impossible? Are we obliged to accept the view, advocated by some thinkers today, that God expects no responsive righteousness from men? That God "breaks through" into human life when and how he will without regard to nature, history, or human understanding? From one who holds this view it is, of course, unreasonable to expect any sense of responsibility for learning to know and do the will of God for his own life or for the life of society. But the Christian has ground for hope that man is capable of active goodness, of useful life with God.

Having acknowledged, in deep humility, his dependence upon God and having accepted with joy and gratitude the plan of salvation which God has freely offered, man has both the privilege and the responsibility of working out his own salvation, as Paul said to the Philippians. As work without faith becomes meaningless routine, so faith without works is dead. Salvation is not a state of being. It represents purposeful activity of God. It is directed toward the achievement of individual goodness on the part of men and social righteousness in communities. It requires of man that he cease to do evil and learn to do good, that he forsake wicked ways and unrighteous thoughts, that he press on to the mark of his high calling.

"Why call ye me, Lord, Lord, and do not the things which I say"? It is a reasonable question and requires a thoughtful answer from men today.

What Does It Mean to Be Good?

How shall we help our children to answer it? All parents and teachers wish their children to "be good." What does it mean to "be good"? How does one decide what is good?

There are situations in the lives of little children in which they must obey promptly and without question but which involve neither "goodness" nor "badness." These are situations which involve physical safety. For example, there is nothing "bad" about striking a match. But little children when they are alone must not strike matches because they do not yet know how to control the fire. Such matters as these require rigid rules, and the rules must be obeyed. They may be explained, but the child should know that he must obey them whether he understands why he is to obey them or not. The list of such rules in the life of any child should be as brief as it is possible to make it consistent with essential physical safety, and prompt punishment should follow violation.

Such matters clearly are in a category of their own, and care should be taken not to confuse them with ethical and spiritual values.

Again, teachers and parents need always to be on guard lest they tend to make their own convenience the criterion for building standards of "goodness" and "badness" for children. Children should learn to have regard for their parents and teachers, just as their parents and teachers have regard for them, as *persons*. Moreover, if their parents and teachers have won the right to confidence and respect, children should be encouraged to show confidence and respect. But it is not "naughty" for a child to sing just because his mother does not wish to have him sing at that moment; it is not "naughty" for him to get dirt on his clean play suit just because his mother wishes him to "look nice" for a visitor. The attitude of parents and other adults sometimes lead children to build a standard of conduct which makes such acts as these serious offenses and leaves unconsidered the really important matters.

What, then, does it mean to live in accordance with the Gospel?

The "sins of the flesh" are surely to be condemned under the query, "Why call ye me Lord, Lord, and do not the things which I say?" Lying, gluttony, impurity, stealing—all such obvious denials of the demands of decent living are banned. But no list of sins to be avoided and virtues to be endorsed can compass the meaning of salvation in one's personal life. The good news of the Gospel is not that a new code of conduct has been given to men, a new set of laws. The ancient Hebrews and the Greek philosophers had laws and ethical codes, and these were not enough. Men became slaves to the letter of the rules, or they became depressed by their inability to live up to the high requirements of the law. The Gospel of Jesus Christ was different. It called men to life with God, to daily conduct, tested not by a rigid law but by the requirements of love in all relationships.

The old law, "an eye for an eye, and a tooth for a tooth," specifically described just what a man might do in retaliation for injury: not more, not less. But according to the Gospel, man is to *do good* to those who injure him. And this because it is the way of God with men.

To one who has committed his way unto the Lord, it is not a rule but the "mind of Christ," the purposes of God as made manifest in Jesus, which is to be determinative. And the "mind of Christ" goes far beyond refraining from sins of the flesh. It gives one a new perspective, a new standard of values, new tastes and desires. It overcomes the spiritual sins: pride, self-centeredness. It leads one to be more than respectable and decent in his personal life. It creates genuine concern for the welfare and happiness of those about him, respect for the personality of others, "doing nothing through faction or through vainglory, but in lowliness of mind each counting other better than himself; not looking each of you to his own things, but each of you also to the things of others."

It will be acknowledged by all thoughtful persons that it is not easy for men to view their own individual conduct as God views it. As has been said, it is not possible for man to know *all* the will of God. Man often sees through a glass, darkly. He will make mistakes so long as he continues his earthly pilgrimage. But it is the Christian faith, supported by the testimony of humble, seeking souls as well as by the saints of all the ages, that man can be made over; that when he seeks God he finds help and guidance, insight and wisdom for meeting the issues of life as they are presented to him; that because he has committed his life to God, he can live that life increasingly in harmony with the will of God. He will go beyond the requirements of the law because love is not bounded by law. He will set his standards of success, not in terms of the requirements of men, but in terms of the purposes of God. He will ask, not, "Will this be applauded?" but, "Will this help persons?"

In spite of the difficulties, then, parents and teachers must cease to do evil, learn to do well. And they must teach their children so to do. Children must be taught to overcome evil thoughts, to restrain harsh words, to avoid selfish conduct. They must be taught to view these matters seriously and to accept responsibility for learning to live above them. They must be taught to cultivate good thoughts, friendly words, generous conduct. And this not in terms of rigid rules but in terms of sincere desire to put themselves in the place of others and know what really *is* kind, friendly conduct in any situation.

Sometimes persons ask God to help them overcome bad habits when really they enjoy the bad habits and wish to continue them; sometimes they ask God to help them learn to control their tempers when really they are rather proud of the reputation for being "high-tempered" and wish to maintain it; sometimes they ask God to help them think of others when really they wish to maintain their present concern for themselves; sometimes they pray, "Thy will be done," when really they wish their own will to be done. Our children must see for themselves how ugly are selfishness, cruelty, greed, and how they bring unhappiness and suffering to men and women and little children; they must see how beautiful are kindness, goodness, love, and how they bring joy and happiness to persons everywhere. Then they may truly repent of their sin and desire to

93

live every day according to the good purposes of God which Jesus showed us.

Children and Social Righteousness

Children must be taught, also, to assume their full measure of responsibility for the social unrighteousness in the community and their full measure of responsibility for overcoming it.

There is much in the life of most American communities and much in the life of our nation of which its citizens may be justly proud and for which they feel deep gratitude. To nurture true love for our country—pride and joy in it and unselfish devotion to it—is the responsibility of every worthy teacher of children. But high patriotism requires of the citizens in a democracy the ability to criticize all those practices which fall short of the best we know; and the Christian religion requires that men and nations alike acknowledge the demands of righteousness. It is our obligation to prepare boys and girls to work, in the name of God, for the correction of practices in the community which hurt persons, all of whom are their brothers, children of their Father. It is our obligation to help them to "make justice the line, and righteousness the plummet" as they begin to evaluate those social and economic and racial and international practices which their experience makes it reasonable for them to consider.

These matters are not so remote from the actual experiences of children as they may seem on first thought. A little child knows about unhappiness that is caused by unwillingness to think of others; he knows about the failure of plans because someone refuses to do his part, to co-operate, to share. When in the experience of the little children situations arise which illustrate the truth that selfishness and greed and injustice make for distress and unhappiness, we should not shrink from so interpreting them.

As children grow older we can help them to understand that careless disregard of the rights of others, whether in games or in using popular books from the public library or in eating a family meal, leads to unpleasantness and the breaking down of satisfactory relationships among persons. Because God is a righteous God and has established the universe upon moral law, unfairness, injustice, selfishness, breed trouble in the human family, whether they are found in the village schoolyard or at an international economic conference. And so man must set himself against such practices wherever they are.

Working for a Better Community

It is not easy to teach these responsibilities to children. In the first place, there is the natural desire on the part of parents and teachers to protect children from ugliness in human relations. We wish they need never know the dark side of our community and national and international life. We have in the past attempted to compromise by planning "sharing enterprises" in the form of Thanksgiving baskets, Christmas toys, missionary scrapbooks, and good will projects, through which we afforded opportunity for dealing with painful problems from a safe distance, as it were. In the midst of the present situation we view these plans with a sort of nostalgia for times-that-are-gone. We know that such simple and pleasant activities, though they may help, are not adequate ways of meeting one's responsibilities as a child of God concerned about his Father's business.

But while we may not protect our children from the world in which they live, we may influence their attitude toward it and their response to it. Clearly, we shall not confront children with awful conditions which they can do nothing to change. To do so is neither sound psychology nor sound religion. But there are bad conditions which children can help to improve.

For example, children of four and five are not too young to become aware of the fact that hunger is a reality in life. They often have pets who have to be fed regularly, or there are babies in the family whose feeding is an event in which the older children take great interest. If food is not provided at the proper times, hunger expresses itself in vocal protest! When, then, they see hungry people outside the home or hear of hungry people or see pictures of hungry people, they may have a basis for the Christian attitude which assumes that *all* persons should be fed so that they may grow strong and that it is the responsibility of those who have food to see that others do not lack food.

As they grow older the interpretation of their enlarging experience should make them increasingly aware of the fact of hunger and what it does to persons. Then we shall come promptly to the question of what we can do about it. Merely taking food to a few persons whom we happen to know is not adequate, though this may be a beginning. We must help our children early to understand that it is not necessary for anyone to be hungry, that God has made available the means of feeding all his children adequately. But he expects us to learn how to use the resources wisely. Our boys and girls must, then, be led to find the causes of hunger, to view them in the light of God's purposes, and to discover some ways in which the causes of hunger can be removed.

Of course, children of six or nine or twelve cannot do a great deal of original research into the causes of hunger or formulate an independent program of action to fight hunger. But they can be related to organizations which have the necessary resources and be related at the level of their own interests and understanding.

The "mind of Christ" reveals also the ugliness of racial discrimination, economic exploitation of defenseless groups, and other practices in a community which may be approved by social custom. Children may learn about the lack of playgrounds, hospitals, and schools for boys and girls of minority groups in their community and may be led to desire to do something to change the conditions.

The Christian churches through increasingly sound and far-reaching social action programs should provide an avenue of approach to all such problems in the communities and opportunity for action on a child level.

Again little children who love and enjoy their church experiences will know at once that children who have no opportunity to go to church are missing something which should be made available to them. Older boys and girls, if they have really experienced for themselves the meaning of the love of God in human life, will eagerly desire to participate in plans to make the Gospel known to others. When undertaken in such spirit, missionary activities become a vital expression of the sense of responsibility to spread abroad the knowledge of the love of God.

Working for a Better World

Few school children of this day are unaware of the devastation that is upon the earth. To attempt to "protect" them from it would mean to isolate them in the remote places of the western desert or the north woods without means of communication or transportation. They cannot live among their fellows and be unaware of the tragic state of man on this planet. Can we, their parents and teachers who believe in God the Father Almighty, the righteous and loving God of the universe, help them to learn from this awful experience of mankind the essential truth that man and nations can achieve their true destiny only in harmony with the eternal purposes of God? Growing boys and girls need to have light thrown upon their own experiences from the experience of the race. They need to see, in a larger setting, the situations which they face. We must help them, as they grow in understanding of geography and of history, to grow also in understanding of their obligations to co-operate in God's righteous purpose for all mankind.

With a sort of spiritual homesickness we look back to the days when we spoke of the time when "wars shall be no more" with full confidence that with our own eyes we would see it come. With a rude awakening we have discovered that our expectations of peace in our time were false. In our disillusionment shall we seek to avoid a repetition of our tragic disappointment by moving to the position that the ideal of a warless world is a mirage on the road of history and that to teach our children to expect and work for a world of peace and brotherhood is foolishness? Or shall we look critically at our former assumptions to see if, perchance, the trouble lay not in our dream but in our failure to understand the conditions under which the dream could be realized?

Those of us who are parents and teachers of children must make up our minds. Our sense of frustration in the present situation, our fears, our indecisions, are being communicated to them. It is not a matter upon which we can delay. The children in the meantime are making up their lives.

We must look squarely at the world as it actually is with eyes wide open to all its problems and yet so guide our children that they may personally experience the meaning of love in the midst of hatred and develop a deep devotion to the will of God which will lead them into a way of life through which just and abiding world peace can come.

In a period when military might is being stressed as never before, when table talk, party talk, playground talk, is dominated by bombers, flying fortresses, destroyers, machine guns, it is not easy to help children think of ways to peace. Yet, whatever may be our view regarding the necessity for temporary concentration upon war in times when aggression flares up and sets the world aflame, there must not be any confusion in the expression of our conviction regarding the will of God that his children live together as brothers nor any holding back in our offering of the full measure of devotion to make his will prevail.

As we look back over the years between the two great world wars, it seems clear that our idea of peace was negative. Peace was *not-war*. It was a state of affairs in which, upon the surface at least, relationships between nations were not disrupted. Now we know that real peace is never negative but that it is positive. It is active good will, out-reaching co-operation. And we have also learned that peace costs something. The strong among the nations must help the weak and not please themselves; resources must be shared on the basis of need rather than taken by nations which can hold them by force. Such bases of peace are clearly in harmony with the will of God as Christians have come to know it, and they must be interpreted to boys and girls.

There was a time when we assumed that singing the songs of children of other lands, playing their games, hearing the stories they love, learning about their festivals and holidays, would teach our children to feel a friendly comradeship with these others from lands far away and would prepare our boys and girls to work with persons of other nations in mutually helpful international relationships. Now we know that we must face many more obstacles to friendship than those differences in language and custom and music.

We are faced with the problem of helping our children to love persons of all nations in spite of conflicting economic interests and clashing national ambitions. And more: we must help them to love persons of other nations in spite of the reports of almost inconceivable brutality, in spite of cruelty and oppression on a scale hitherto unknown. We must look at the facts, not evade them. And we must look at all the facts. As they grow older, can we lead our boys and girls soberly to consider the responsibility of our own nation for international disorder? Can we help them to look at the social and individual sins of our own people as factors in world catastrophe? Can we lead them to a sense of sincere repentance even in this day?

Let us remind ourselves again: *Peace costs something.* There can be no peace in the world until there are persons who have learned through experience the way of peace as the way of doing the will of God, the way of real brotherhood, the way of self-forgetful love, the way of bearing one another's burdens, the way of preferring one another. Thus to learn the way of peace means that in every situation in which we have influence we will spare ourselves no effort and no sacrifice to realize this way of life.

In our homes and churches we will seek to create a genuine fellowship of love. In our communities we will relentlessly search for the facts regarding the needs of children and boys and girls and men and women. And

100

having learned the facts, we will consider how we should view them as children of God, what we should do about them, no matter what it may cost us in the way of comfort or social prestige or financial strain. For is it reasonable to think that nations can learn to work together in ways to avoid economic and racial and social and ideological conflicts which lead to war unless small groups within one community can solve problems in these areas? It is reasonable to think that nations can learn to deal without war with wrongdoers and unpopular and belligerent members of the family of nations unless the Christians within one community can work constructively on the problem of helping those who are delinquent to re-enter the fellowship of the community as contributing members?

If we really wish to teach our children and our boys and girls to make a contribution toward world peace, we will, then, have to *work* at it, beginning with the problem closest at hand which is causing friction, injustice, suffering to persons, and doing something to solve that problem in accordance with the will of God revealed to us in Jesus Christ.

Through addressing ourselves specifically to those situations in which we can actually make a difference, through relieving suffering, sharing pain, resolving conflicts, removing injustice, we may experience for ourselves and help our children to experience a sense of peace, the sort of peace of which Jesus spoke when he said, "My peace I give unto you." He was not speaking of ease or comfort or release from the hardships of life. He was speaking rather of an inner peace that comes from wholehearted commitment to the will of God, an utter devotion of all one's capacities toward the realization of his good purposes in one's own life and in society no matter what the cost

101

in suffering, loneliness, persecution. Persons in whom this peace dwells are, in the present world tragedy, the only hope of world healing. Perhaps slowly, but surely, their influence will spread, and a real, not a superficial, peace will ultimately come to the world. This peace will not be maintained by force, as was the peace of the Roman Empire. It will not be maintained by economic pressures, as was the precarious peace between the two world wars of our day. It will be, rather, a peace that will endure because it is rooted in the righteousness and love of God and in responsive love and righteousness among his children of all nations.

With God and the Minority

To lead our children in the way of utter devotion to the will of God in their personal lives and in all their human relationships will not be easy either for their teachers or for the children. It is not likely to be a popular way. It will call for willingness to give up ambitions which are generally approved, ambitions to achieve financial success, a place of importance in the community life. It is likely to involve them in conflict with the majority of the community in which they live. Those who love children shrink from putting them in a position which involves such risks. Because of this fact, probably, more than any other, there has been reluctance to face squarely the practical day-by-day demands of wholehearted discipleship to Jesus Christ.

Many persons who in their maturity see clearly that Jesus was right and who feel a great yearning to follow him unreservedly are hindered by the thought of what such a way of life on their part would require of their children. They wish their children to "have everything," meaning, primarily, to have a place of prestige within their group. But is this attitude really a sound one? Does it not indicate that we are unwilling to trust our children to the love of God, that we think our way will afford them something better than the way of God has to offer them?

It must be said definitely that this way of devotion to the will of God will not be a way of comfort and ease. It has never been, throughout history. Those who elect to follow it elect to stand *with God and the minority*. It has always been so. This way led Jesus to the Cross. It has led many of his most devoted followers into personal suffering and disaster. And yet, as we view the way of devotion to the will of God against the background of history, it becomes clear that it is the only way whereby men and nations can be saved—the only way that brings abiding joy and true happiness to men individually or in communities. St. Augustine was right when he said, "Thou hast made us for thyself, O God; and our souls are restless until they find their rest in thee." The testimony is clear. The men who have left, in history and in literature, the record of the happy life, the life of blessedness have been the *good* men.

We must face the fact, then, that we are not educating our children for a life of comfortable mediocrity, of easy conformity to the popularly accepted customs and standards of their day. We are educating them for life with God. We are striving to help them take their place as true sons of their Father—"children of God . . . . in the midst of a crooked and perverse generation."

IX

The Neglected Children

THERE ARE NOT MANY ACCOUNTS IN THE GOSPELS of Jesus' direct contact with children. But in all the incidents recorded there is the clear indication that Jesus was especially kind and gracious to them as persons and that he considered children eager, responsive candidates for discipleship. There is also clear indication that Jesus was stirred to indignation by those who would hinder the development of little children.

"Forbid Them Not"

When his own disciples so far misunderstood his spirit as to think that he was too busy to be concerned with children and rebuked the mothers who had brought them to receive his blessing, "Jesus was moved with indignation, and said unto them, Suffer the little children to come unto me; forbid them not!" Again, when he had called a little child to him, he said: "Whoso shall receive one such little child in my name receiveth me: but whoso shall cause one of these little ones that believe on me to stumble, it is profitable for him that a great millstone should be hanged about his neck, and that he should be sunk in the depth of the sea."

These are words as strong as almost any of the recorded words of Jesus. He was deeply offended by the neglect or the positive interference which would keep little children from the fellowship in the Kingdom of God which he believed to be the purpose of God for them all. Indeed, he said explicitly, "It is not the will of your Father who is in heaven, that one of these little ones should perish."

In previous chapters we have been considering, primarily, approaches to children who are within the fellowship of the Christian Church and whose parents are concerned for their spiritual welfare. But there are millions of other children—children who are being handicapped by the conditions under which they are forced to live—in whose way "stumbling blocks" are being placed by their environment or by careless or evil adults. Some of the general situations which hurt children have been mentioned. It seems necessary, however, to deal with them more in detail. What are some of the situations responsible for "forbidding" millions of children to respond to the invitation of Jesus? To what extent must the present mature members of the Christian fellowship in the earth bear responsibility for these situations?

Conditions Which Are Hurting Children

There is available a recent comprehensive survey of the condition of children in the United States through the reports of the White House Conference on Children in a Democracy, in which workers in all phases of child welfare participated. There are no groups in our country who should have a greater interest in these findings than the Christian Church.[1]

What does the report show? First of all, that the largest percentage of children in the United States are living in the areas and in the families which have the lowest income. The result is that good schools, good medical care, good housing, good recreational facilities, good churches—all these essentials for conserving child

[1] A summary of the findings of this conference is available from the Children's Bureau, Washington, D. C.

life—are least available where there are the largest number of children to need them. There is a direct relationship between the lack of these facilities and unwholesome child development.

In health it is most obvious. For example, the tuberculosis rate varies widely among communities only a few miles apart. In communities affording good living conditions it is one-third to one-half what it is in congested, poorly housed areas.

More starkly revealing is the fact that the death rate among babies and among children under fifteen years of age rises steadily from locality to locality as one moves from privileged to underprivileged communities. In the case of some diseases of childhood, a child living in one neighborhood of a given city has just half the chance to get well that a child in another neighborhood has. In terms of cold figures, children in families whose income is less than $800 a year have one chance in ten to recover from some diseases, while children in the same communities but in families whose income is $2500 a year have nine chances out of ten—the difference being due to the fact that in one case the resources of medical science are *not* made available, and in the other case they *are* made available. In the case of infant mortality, competent medical authorities say that one half the 120,000 babies who die annually in the United States could be saved if medical care were available.[2]

The White House Conference Report places large emphasis upon the family as the fundamental social unit, the one which is most likely to be determinative in the child's personality development, and stresses the importance of keeping the family stable as the most important

---

[2] From the *Report of the Technical Committee on Medical Care*, Washington, D. C., 1938.

service which can be rendered to children. Yet there are thousands of children who do not have a stable family life due to social and economic causes which could be prevented if they were attacked by persons of intelligence and good will. In other cases there is insecurity which is caused by broken homes. The increase of divorce in America presents a serious problem to the Christian community and lays upon children a burden beyond their strength. Even where there is no actual breakup of the family, there is often disharmony and lack of understanding and sympathy which cause children bewilderment and unhappiness.

Another problem which has been lifted up is that of children in minority groups. The report shows that these children in America live under serious special handicaps. The brave declaration adopted at the end of the Children's Charter of 1930, "For every child these rights, regardless of race or color or creed wherever he may live under the protection of the American flag," [3] has not represented the majority sentiment in our country during the years that have followed its adoption. The approximately thirteen million children in our country who are other than native-born white children of native parentage have not shared equally in the privileges made available by community, state, and national, sources. Many children in minority groups are segregated educationally, and these segregated schools are, for the most part, far behind the schools provided for the majority groups. Similarly, recreational facilities are not available. Worst of all, there is the emotional handicap of knowing that one is being discriminated against.

It is not surprising that a definite relation has been

[3] *Report of the White House Conference on Child Health and Protection,* Department of the Interior, Washington, D. C., 1930.

established between all these conditions we have been reviewing and juvenile delinquency. Family dislocation, community neglect of opportunities for wholesome recreation, bad housing, inadequate provision for health care, bad community life, discrimination—all these conditions are contributing to the growth of juvenile delinquency. In a recent address J. Edgar Hoover said, "Persons who are little more than boys and girls committed thirteen per cent of our murders; twenty-eight per cent of our robberies; forty-one per cent of our burglaries: and fifty-one per cent of our automobile thefts. To me it is a matter of grave concern."

Salvation and the Child's Present Life

To all those who bear the name of Jesus Christ it should be more than a matter of grave concern. It should be cause for sincere repentance. "Whosoever shall cause one of these little ones . . . . to stumble!" Let the little children come, *"and forbid them not."* Their bodies stunted or in pain; their minds filled with ugliness and confusion; their spirits crushed by unkindness, neglect, loneliness, unfair discrimination—how hard it is for them to hear the voice of God! How difficult it is for them to find the way in which he would have them walk!

There are millions of children in our country desperately in need of the active help of Christians in changing conditions which are hindering in gross and preventable fashion their wholesome development.

Beyond our own country are millions more, overwhelmed by the calamities of a war for which they bear no responsibility, terrified by cruelties, brutalities, destruction, on a scale never known before in human history. What chance do they have for responding to the love and righteousness of God with answering love and

108

righteousness? How can they come to know the Gospel?

There can be no doubt that here we are faced with one of the most profoundly disturbing problems in understanding the plan of salvation. There need be no doubt at the point of God's love—his seeking, yearning, suffering love. There need be no doubt of the sufficiency of the Gospel of Jesus Christ to meet the needs of all men and women and little children everywhere. But how can the stumbling blocks be removed so that these children may understand and accept the plan of salvation? How can the conditions which have *forbidden* them be overcome? Through no fault of their own millions of children have had no opportunity to hear of the love of God, to come to experience the comfort and the courage which it affords to his children. It seems clear that Jesus was not unmindful of those who would live in such conditions. And he laid upon his followers solemn responsibility to care for them.

Jesus said that he was come to seek and to save those who were lost. And certainly his followers can do no less than to carry on his work. But all too often those who would save men go about it as if the human soul were quite independent of its earthly environment. They believe, as Dr. Ernest F. Tittle points out, that God cares profoundly for the human soul but is not very much concerned about the conditions in which the soul lives; for it is assumed that social conditions of whatever kind can neither promote nor obstruct the soul's salvation. They believe that salvation is directed exclusively toward the future life; that God is

concerned only to deliver men from the toils of an earthly existance and to prepare them for entrance into that unseen world of the spirit where alone his kingdom is or ever can be. . . . God is not greatly concerned about the external conditions of their [men's] pilgrimage, whether there be freedom or bondage, justice or injustice, peace or war. Under any conditions, is not his grace sufficient to deliver the trusting soul from its earthly foes and to secure for it some blessed foretaste of eternal bliss? [4]

And so such persons undertake to "explain the plan of salvation" to neglected children without concerning themselves with their tragic need for friendship, human understanding, relief from awful insecurity.

This view of salvation is held by many devout persons today. Comfortably placed persons too often hold on to it as a way of escaping the necessity of changing conditions which are hurting. They say that nothing is too hard for God, that he can and will save the poor and the downtrodden if and when he will, that their present state has nothing at all to do with the matter. They can, therefore, in good conscience participate in, or contribute to, the work of "saving souls" without "meddling with" social and economic factors in the lives of those they seek to save.

Some, on the other hand, who are themselves the poor and underprivileged, embrace this view of salvation because they have become utterly discouraged about this life, have given up any hope of justice or fulfillment. They have pushed all their hopes ahead to the future life, when they will live in "Beulah Land," when they will no longer struggle with hunger, because they will feast "on the manna from the bountiful supply," when they will hear "far away the noise of strife" but feel secure in the thought that none of it will longer trouble them because they are safe "within the harbor of God's love."

Shall we, then, separate the needs of children for health and human friendship and understanding from their need

[4] *Christians in an Unchristian Society,* Association Press, 1939, pp. 4-5.

of salvation and try to save their souls while we ignore their bodies? Let us look to Jesus for guidance.

The Concern of Jesus for Man's Life

When he came to Nazareth and went to the synagogue, Jesus read this passage from Isaiah:

> The Spirit of the Lord is upon me,
> Because he anointed me to preach good tidings to the poor;
> He hath sent me to proclaim release to the captives,
> And recovering of sight to the blind,
> To set at liberty them that are bruised.

Again, in the disturbing passage regarding man's judgment before God, he describes the separation of the blessed as based upon these experiences: "For I was hungry, and ye gave me to eat; I was thirsty, and ye gave me drink; I was a stranger, and ye took me in; naked, and ye clothed me; I was sick, and ye visited me; I was in prison, and ye came unto me."

In his life and ministry Jesus did not dismiss as unimportant hunger and sickness, loneliness and despair on the part of men. He did not pass by on the other side when men were bruised and deserted. He did not view without concern the selfish comfort of the rich and the bitter want of the poor.

The record is clear. We believe that Jesus revealed God to men; and Jesus spent many weary hours ministering to the physical needs of men. The God and Father of our Lord Jesus Christ is not too great to be *good*, to care about his children, to strive mightily to help them— and that in all phases of life where they have need. And he expects us to work with him.

111

What Is Required?

In the situation which confronts us we may not meet our responsibility by feeling distressed or even by sending a check. Nor can we escape the situation by denouncing persons or institutions or community habits. Hating, and declaiming against, evil may relieve our emotional strains, but it does not help the victims of evil. We may meet our responsibilities only by learning to be good workmen who know how to change conditions in accordance with the will of God made known to us in Jesus Christ. There must be on the part of intelligent, devout Christians cordial co-operation with the community agencies working for child health and child welfare. In many communities these agencies are working against a load of public indifference which thwarts them at every turn. Upon Christian citizens is laid the obligation to know what these organizations are planning, to evaluate their work, and to support wholeheartedly all the constructive efforts in the community making for better conditions for children and boys and girls.

There must be on the part of the Christian citizens the demand that young offenders be dealt with in ways that will *save* them, not condemn them. In this realm good intentions are not enough. Some young offenders are *serious* offenders; they are at odds with society. They require skilled and specialized attention if they are to be made candidates for good citizenship. Good will is not enough; good will must be supported by technical service. But technical service must also be supported by good will. Unless these young offenders have some sense of fellowship, some feeling of belonging, some awareness of concern for them, the best technical skill is not likely to be enough. In dealing with physical illness, the doctors report that it is only the patient who *wants* to get well—

112

who feels that it is *worth while* to struggle against the disease—who makes rapid and lasting recovery. In the realm of serious social and emotional disturbances, it is even more important that the patient have a feeling that it is worth while to overcome the attitudes and habits which have brought him into conflict with society. He needs to feel that there is a supporting fellowship ready to help him: to be patient with him, to love him even in spite of unresponsiveness, unattractiveness, and maladjustment to the life of the new group in which he finds himself. Only so can he have hope and gain confidence and achieve success in becoming a good citizen.

The Responsibility of the Church

Is the fellowship of the Christian Church showing concern for these children who are in such great need? Verbally, yes; actually, only in a restricted way. By and large, the members of Christian churches do not feel *responsible* for the conditions which are causing children to stumble. They do not respond cordially to sermons or to programs which seek to enlist their active concern. They do not wish to face the conditions which are causing distress to children and to study hard enough to understand them and to know what is the wisest way to deal with them. They do not care to be "involved" in campaigns to secure playgrounds in crowded areas, to require condemnation proceedings against housing that is breeding sickness, to remove discriminations against minority groups in the health and educational facilities made available to the children of the communities.

What is the responsibility of local churches for unchurched children? Do they feel responsible for attempting to relate the children of the community to the churches? Do the churches *want* all the children to come?

113

In a recent conference one of the workers, in speaking to some such question as this, said, "I know why the children who are unchurched in my community do not come to our church. We do not want them. That is the real truth of the matter. These 'outside' children often have bad manners; they do not know how to behave in church; they are religiously illiterate; and if they came to our church they would spoil our smoothly running program."

In how many local churches does this attitude prevail? In how many local churches is there such burning desire to seek and to save the children of the community that no amount of study and work and discouragement—and the task will involve all this—is too much?

We who lay claim to our sonship to God may not rest in a situation which spells misery and frustration for millions of little children. We may not be content with a formal call to children to repent of their sins and accept God's promise of salvation in some future state. We know through the revelation of God in Jesus that it is not the will of God for such conditions to continue; we know that God is working to overcome them. We know he is depending upon us to help him. We cannot look on these present conditions and do nothing to change them—"unless," as Dr. Tittle tells us, "we are capable of deserting and betraying God."

x

The Bible and Children

IN WHAT WAYS IS THE BIBLE A "SPECIAL" BOOK? Why is it that we consider it much more important to teach our children the Bible than to acquaint them with other ancient literature and ancient history?

Of course the obvious answer is: "Because the Bible is the word of God." And that answer is true. But it may be also rather ambiguous. What does it mean to us as we say it? Is it just a phrase which we have heard; or is it a shibboleth; or is it the expression of a deep-seated conviction, rooted in personal experience?

The Bible As the Word of God

The Bible is the word of God to those who through it hear God speak to them. It is the word of God to those who, giving themselves diligently to its study and meditating upon its sayings, enter into the experience it portrays of the great souls who struggle and triumph and receive growing insight into the purposes of God. It is the word of God to those who find in it understanding of the meaning of life and strength and courage to meet life.

What we are saying is that the text of the Bible as we hold it in our hands may or may not be the word of God to men. The Bible is not the word of God to men so long as it remains unopened on the living room table or in the church school library. It is not the word of God to men so long as it is read perfunctorily or quoted in or out of context in order to win an argument. It is not the word of God when it is used as a sort of "magic," as, for instance, when one expects to find the answer to a question by opening the pages at random and accepting as the "answer" the first verse upon which the eyes fall.

That is, so far as we have any understanding of the way God speaks to his children—understanding which has come to us through our own experience, through the experiences of great souls down the ages, supremely through the experiences of Jesus—so far as we have any understanding through all these sources of the way God speaks, we can say that the word of God may not be expected to come to his children in these ways. Rather, the experience of the race seems to tell us that God speaks to his children when they listen for his guidance, when they are faced with problems or decisions beyond their powers, when they are aware of their need of him, when they have acknowledged the sins which have been keeping them from being able to hear him, when they are ready to heed his word, when their hearts are full of joy and gratitude which they wish to express. If they study the Bible in such a spirit they may expect confidently that it will become in their own personal experience, as it has in the experience of others, the word of God.

They may not find right away, plainly stated, the exact answer to the specific problems of life which they face. Rather, the rank and file of seeking souls have found that with each passing year spent in the study of the Bible there have come more and more clearly the answers to the great problems and the questions which face human beings. They have found that there have come convictions regarding the *direction* life must take in all its specific relationships, regarding the standards which enable one to decide between greater and lesser values. Yes, God speaks to men through the Bible when they have prepared

116

themselves to understand the language in which he speaks.

We wish our children to know the Bible, then, because in a unique fashion this great Book may become for them in very truth the word of God.

Helping Children to Know the Bible

How can we, parents and teachers of children, help our children to know the Bible? There was a time when we would feel that we had the answer when we replied that we must see to it that they know the stories of the Bible; that they learn their memory verses; and that, as they grow older, they be given help in choosing passages for daily Bible reading. In the more serious mood of the present time, when we are so deeply aware of our need for help in understanding our world and God's purposes, we are realizing that this is not enough.

Even before they hear Bible stories and long before they hear any discussion of the nature and teachings of the Bible, little children can begin to feel a sense of the special significance of this book. They can observe their parents reading it silently or aloud to one another and to the older children. They can feel that this book has special meaning, is of special value, to their parents. When they first go to Sunday school, they can hear their teacher refer to it or see her handle it as a book which is especially precious and beloved. They can hear simple, beautiful verses read from the book. After a while they can hear stories which come from the Bible. And so, before they have any definite teaching about the Bible, they may have formed an attitude of expectancy toward it.

At this point, when we are ready to begin the more systematic attempt to relate our children personally to the nature and the message of the Bible, we may take any

117

one of several different ways of approaching our opportunity.

These different approaches may be pretty well grouped under two major procedures. We may begin with the content of the Bible and ask: What does it say to us? Or we may begin with the need and experiences of children and ask: What guidance does the Bible offer for these specific needs and experiences? Neither of these, of course, really excludes the other.

Studying the Content of the Bible

Most parents and teachers wish their children to know the content of the Bible. There is general agreement that the Bible is the treasury of the world's greatest religious literature, preserving the religious heritage of the race as no other literature does. It is therefore important for all persons in present-day situations to know the great teachings and the great characters found in the Bible. It is important because only in the light of the past can we interpret the present. It is important because it provides a basis of unity and understanding among persons of faiths widely differing.

But there are several points of view from which this literature is taught. Some teachers emphasize the appreciation of selected portions of the Bible as literature and as the record of the experience of the race, not attempting primarily to find in it guidance for present, specific experience, but rather primarily to understand what it meant to the persons out of whose experience it came. Thus, they would not be concerned with finding from the life of Abraham some specific incident which might be used for purposes of present-day morals, such as the story of his sharing with Lot. They would rather tell the story in its broad sweep to help the children to see Abraham in his own setting, with his own limitations and his own failures, and to understand something of his own struggle and dawning insight and what God meant to him.

An approach which at the outset disavows any purpose of "pointing a moral" will permit teachers and children more fully to enjoy the Bible, to wonder about its stories of extraordinary events, to feel the thrill of the great stories of adventure, to lose themselves in the majestic rhythm of the Psalms. Children need increased opportunity thus to enjoy the Bible.

This point of view is presented as one which would make it possible to teach the Bible in the public schools. It would be strictly unsectarian. But it would acquaint children with the content of the Bible.

But the teaching of the Bible as literature is, of course, not enough if we wish it to be the word of God to our children. Most teachers and parents feel that, in addition to being great literature, the stories and history and poetry and prophecies of the Bible are of high religious significance which, if wisely taught to children and growing boys and girls, will reveal to them the will of God. This point of view calls for the development of a graded plan for studying the Bible so that its content may be known thoroughly, and its message may be related to present-day living of growing persons.

There is another quite different point of view regarding the teaching of Bible content. It holds that each word is the word of God and therefore necessary to man's spiritual life. Those who hold this view are concerned that the child should be familiar with the content of all the books of the Bible, and they consider it their responsibility to see that he studies them all, chapter by chapter, as he grows from childhood into youth. They interpret the saying, "Thy word have I hid in my heart that I might not sin against thee," to mean that if a large amount of biblical material is memorized, children will have with them always a shield against temptation. They feel that teaching the child to know the content of the Bible *is* teaching him the Christian religion.

This point of view gives a sense of security, and opportunity to rest upon authority. And, indeed, if it is diligently carried out over a number of years, the boy or girl will be familiar with the content of the Bible. But will the Bible have entered into the experience of the children so that it becomes for them the word of God? Simply to know the content of the Bible is not an adequate way to hear the voice of God.

Teaching the Bible Through Relating It Directly to Experience

The experience-centered approach to the study of the Bible begins, not with a body of material, but with the lives of present-day persons. It proposes to help persons to know, and to carry out in everyday living, God's purposes for their lives and the lives of others by helping them, first, to understand their own situations and experiences and relationships and, then, to find in the Bible guidance for meeting these situations and experiences and relationships. The Bible is the primary source book of religious education because the Bible interprets the will of God as no other book does. But the Bible is used in relation to the experience of growing persons rather than being taught in historical sequence or portion by portion.

Thus, one does not start out to teach the story of the Good Samaritan as Bible content. Rather, one finds that children around seven years of age, let us say, need help in improving their relationships with persons of other races in their community. One turns to the Bible to find

120

the best material, within the understanding of seven-year-olds, which will help them to recognize and to desire to change their careless or unkind attitudes. The story of the Good Samaritan is selected for this purpose. Or, one finds that Junior boys and girls need a deepened sense of the presence of God in the world, of his care and concern for his children. Possible biblical material is considered to meet this need, and Psalm 121 is selected in the expectation that as children hear the ancient Hebrews singing their confidence in the goodness and power of God, the present-day children will enter into this experience and feel their own faith in God's care strengthened.

This is the point of view which has been to a greater or less extent used in our recent graded lessons. It is not, of course, divorced from teaching Bible content. All these courses have units on specific Bible content, such as: "The Life of Jesus," "Heroes of Israel." But they also have units on "Learning to Play Happily Together," "Living at Our Best," "Understanding Our World," "Being a Good Neighbor." All these units use material from the Bible, but it is selected from different parts of the record and brought together around the experiences and relationships of growing persons. This plan makes more immediately available to children the help which the Bible affords on specific problems with which they are faced. It facilitates the "making of connections," so to speak, between the Bible and the present-day needs of growing persons. And so it is likely to help children to recognize in the Bible a source of help and guidance, to find that through it God does speak to them.

But because the material is selected from various parts of the Bible and brought together around experiences of persons, the child may get a fragmentary idea of the Bible. For example, we bring together around the child's experiences in learning to live happily with others such material as "Abraham Shares with Lot," "Lydia, a Helper," "Rebecca and the Tired Traveler," "Elisha's Room on the Roof," "The Good Samaritan," "Isaac and the Wells." All these stories are unified in the experience of the child. But they are not related to the context in which they occur in the Bible, and so their full meaning is not interpreted. This limitation should be corrected with later studies of connected portions of the Bible.

Changing Attitud. Toward the Bible

We have been attempting to describe several attitudes toward teaching the Bible which are found among large numbers of Chistian teachers. Almost all of them have something which we concede as a value and something which we concede as a limitation.

There has, it seems clear, been a marked change in the attitude of men generally toward the Bible during recent years. Following the Reformation, the study of the Bible was regarded as the primary source of understanding of God and his purposes. It was therefore, a matter of tremendous importance that everyone know the Bible. It was taught diligently to little children and growing boys and girls, and it was read and pondered by adults. It was not questioned; it was accepted.

With the development of scholarship which raised certain questions regarding the authorship of books of the Bible, the reliability of the texts of some portions of the Bible, and the dependability of translations, the confidence of common men in the absolute authority of the Bible was shaken. And with the rise of science and of interest in man's own abilities to understand the universe and use it, his sense of great need for the comfort and insight which he had found in the Bible diminished.

122

Gradually, then, there was less emphasis upon teaching the content of the Bible to children. There has never been a time in Christian churches when the Bible was *ignored,* but many other materials came to be included along with it, and there was less concentration upon the centrality of its message. In many churches it came to be regarded as one among many sources of materials which stimulate religious insight and inspiration—an important one always, but not above comparison with other materials. Certain significant passages were selected for children, and these were carefully taught; but it was not considered of any great importance that boys and girls be familiar with the content of the Bible as a whole.

Now there appears to be a definite tendency to reinstate the content of the Bible in the place of primary importance in religious education. This is due in part to the sense of fear and awful uncertainty in the face of the present situation within which men live. Men yearn for some authority, something tangible to which they can hold for reassurance and comfort. And so they are turning again to the "greathearted Book" of the ages as the word of God speaking to them. But it is due also in part to a new sense of humility on the part of men. They are recognizing their own limitations; they are seeking insight greater than their own.

We must approach the increased opportunity to help children appreciate and use the Bible with sincere purpose to find in the Bible resources which will really make a difference in their lives. We shall resist any effort to make it an escape from the necessity for thought and hard work, on the one hand, and to make it a support for weird doctrines on the other. This means that we must recognize first of all the need of *studying* the Bible ourselves. We must know its content and we must seek to understand its message.

Toward Understanding the Bible

If the Bible is to speak to us today, we must, of course, recognize that the text which we use is not the original text but a translation. We shall, therefore, make use of several translations to help us understand in English the meaning of the phrases used in the ancient languages. There are several recent translations which throw a great deal of light upon the meaning of certain passages by using a more modern form of the English language than was used in the King James translation, made over three hundred years ago. Those who cling to the King James translation for its beauty and loftiness of expression will, when seeking to understand what the Bible says, use some more recent translation for clarification.[1]

Then we shall recognize that the writers through whom God spoke had certain human limitation. They lived under certain social conditions, and in a specific period of history. If their messages were to have any meaning to their contemporary hearers, they must, of necessity, use the thought forms and assume the social background which these hearers knew. But the thought forms and the social background of the men and women of ancient Palestine and the Roman Empire are not our thought forms nor our social background. Consequently, we find some of the sayings puzzling. In the Old Testament plural marriages and slavery and despotic forms of government seem to have been taken for granted. Certainly

---

[1] Among the helpful translations into modern English are:
E. J. Goodspeed, *The Bible: an American Translation*
James Moffatt, *The Bible: A New Translation*
R. G. Moulton, *The Modern Reader's Bible*

we shall not assume that because the ancient Hebrews took them for granted and referred to them in the Bible, these customs are part of God's purposes for his children.

It was not until many hundred years later that man discovered that the world was round; so to the Bible writers it was quite reasonable to refer to the four corners of the earth. This does not mean that we shall have to contend that the earth *does have* four corners and teach our children so. And so we might go on. All this sort of interpretation interferes with our hearing the voice of God as he speaks to us through the Bible. Instead, let us accept the facts in the case and teach our children to do so.

Again, we shall recognize that the Bible tells about persons who were very good and persons who were very bad, and persons in between. And the fact that a person appears in the Bible record as a leader is no reason for assuming that he was good. A great deal of quite unnecessary confusion has arisen from the attempts of present-day teachers to make some very earthy Old Testament characters into Christian saints.

We shall recognize, too, that some parts of the Bible are of more religious value than others. We shall not, for example, expect of Abraham the same high level of understanding of God and his purposes that we expect of Hosea; nor consider equally important the detailed laws of Leviticus and the exhortations of Isaiah; nor put the same confidence in the ethical standards of David as we put in those of Amos. We shall, moreover, always approach the Old Testament through the New Testament, recognizing that the revelation of God and his purposes in Jesus Christ is the fullest revelation.

There are some portions of the Old Testament which we shall not attempt to teach to boys and girls. These are the portions which deal with manners and customs which have been superseded and which reflect thoughts of God which Jesus clearly set aside. For example, Samson's prayer, "O Lord Jehovah, remember me, I pray thee, and strengthen me, I pray thee, only this once, O God, that I may be at once avenged of the Philistines for my two eyes," is in marked contrast to the prayer of Jesus, "Father, forgive them; for they know not what they do." Except for purposes of contrast, therefore, we shall not emphasize the story of Samson.

There are some parts even of the New Testament which are very difficult for laymen, of the present day to understand. The meaning is obscured because the thought forms are unfamiliar to us. This is notably true of some of the Epistles and of such books as Revelation. Often there is help available in lesson periodicals or in special books which we use for our own Bible study. But often we feel that we are not getting very much from some portions of the Bible. Would it not be the part of wisdom to recognize that we ourselves have certain limitations, just as the Old Testament characters had? As they often failed to understand when God spoke to them, so we may expect to be unable to comprehend fully and all at once his messages to us. And so we shall not fret about it! We shall accept the fact of our limitations, not in resignation, but in humility, knowing that our present blindness need not be permanent and that gradually we shall understand more and more and more of the heights and the depths of the spiritual truths in the Bible. In the meantime, we shall feed our souls on those portions which we can understand, ordering our lives in accordance with their teachings, and encouraging our children to share our appreciation.

126

Children and the Bible

The various lesson materials prepared by the denominations for the use of the churches recognize the circumstances which we have been reviewing and attempt to meet them. They do not propose that children and boys and girls be introduced to *all* the Bible. They take account of the limitations of the children and of the fact that some passages are of higher religious value in growing life than are other passages. Becauses of the limited time available in the church school, they endeavor to select for use with children those passages which so far as the experience of Christians through the years has any light to throw on the question, seem to be the passages which afford the best approach to an understanding of the message of the Bible.

These passages are, for the most part, the narrative and the poetic passages, with some use of the maxims of the ancient wise men and of the sayings of Jesus and of Paul. That is, the accounts in the Bible of the actual experiences of men: how they felt about God and about their fellow men, how the thought of the presence of God helped them in meeting the issues of life, their successes and their failures in living with their friends and their enemies— these concrete narrative portions are most likely to help the children feel that the Bible is a book which they can understand and love and enjoy. Summaries of ways of acting, such as: "Forget not to show love unto strangers"; "Love your enemies, do good to them that hate you"; "As ye would that men should do to you, do ye also to them likewise"; "It is an honor for a man to cease from strife: but every fool will be meddling"—such summaries will be used to help the children reach some definite conclusions, "put some pegs down," so to speak, in their personal program of everyday living.

127

Moreover, in selecting material to use with children, we shall recognize the fact that many passages may be used for a partial interpretation—passages which we shall wait until later years to interpret more fully. For example, it is unlikely that the 23rd Psalm can be readily understood as a Psalm of God's love for men until boys and girls have some ability to interpret figures of speech, that is, about the time they are in junior high school. But children much younger can love this Psalm as a beautiful poem of the care of a shepherd for his flock, and it can be so used with them, illustrated with pictures. If there is an attempt to force the more mature interpretation, the child will likely only become confused and feel that the Psalm is alien and strange. But if we leave it as a poem of a kind shepherd, he will have a friendly, appreciative attitude toward it and will build up a background of understanding which will enable him to find in it rich and deeply satisfying religious significance as he comes later to see its full meaning.

In some of the narratives we shall not tell all the story. But we shall always be scrupulously careful to tell the story truly so far as we do tell it. That is, while we may select a single incident from a long narrative, the parts we do tell must be such that they can be fitted into the whole later on without jolts and jars. For example, we shall not tell—as one lesson course once did—the story of Jacob's leaving home as an occasion of happy family preparation for a journey on the part of one of its members, with fond farewells and best wishes!

But we shall not confine ourselves to isolated incidents from the lives of great leaders and teachers. By the time a child is seven or eight years of age, he is ready for some brief biographies of these great personalities, a series of connected stories, selected so as to give something of a total impression of the personality. These first biographical studies should be simple, dealing primarily with the activities of the persons rather than with his thoughts, but should result in some feeling of definite acquaintance on the part of the child. Jesus is likely to be the first of these biographical studies, with Moses, David, Joseph, and Paul being selected soon after.

As the boys and girls grow older and begin to understand something of the sweep of history, there should be provided ample opportunity for a survey of the history of the nations as it is recorded in the Bible. The purpose of such a survey should not be to teach the names of the kings of Israel and of Judah in their order, nor to make a chart of the principal happenings during the reign of each one. Rather, our purpose should be a religious purpose—the purpose of helping boys and girls to see the righteous judgment of God in history. We have not, for the most part, provided adequate help at this point in our program of religious education. The study should show how the nations sinned, how they suffered for their sins, how through it all God loved them and forgave them but did not abrogate the moral law of the universe to enable them to escape the consequences of their sin. Our boys and girls need to see without ambiguity or obscurity the operation of this law. The historical books of the Old Testament afford this opportunity as does no other body of material. Such a survey also shows man's growing understanding of God and his purposes.

Of course, this sort of study requires a great deal more in the way of preparation on the part of the teachers than does the preparation, week by week, of a lesson based upon a brief passage. But it is absolutely necessary if we are really to help our boys and girls hear the voice of God speaking through the Bible.

During these years, too, will come the more complete studies of the life of Jesus, leading to an understanding of his mission and a personal experience of commitment to discipleship.

In the high school years there should come a serious study of the high teachings of the prophets, of the teachings of Jesus, and of the teachings of Paul. These materials, by their form as well as by their content, are difficult for younger children to appreciate. They require a certain amount of experience in living to be most meaningful. In the stories of what Jesus *did* and what his followers *did* we shall of course have introduced the children to what Jesus taught about the good life, the life of man with God. But in these later years we shall consider directly the teachings themselves and shall attempt to lead present-day young people to a real understanding of the demands they make upon persons and the high joys they offer.

Interspersed through all these studies of the Bible there must be units which will help boys and girls to know something about the Bible as a collection of books, how it came to be, how the various books came together, how the translations were made, and so on. When the children first begin to read the Bible for themselves, probably about the fourth or fifth grade, there should come the first of these units, the purpose of which will be to acquaint the child with the physical make-up of the Bible so he can find passages in it. A few years later there may come a unit on how the Bible came to be and its translation into the languages of the world. And in high school years there may come a more detailed study of the formation of the canon and the influence of the Bible upon the nations.

The Purpose of Teaching the Bible to Children

Are we, then, advocating a "content" approach to the Bible? In a sense, yes. But not in the sense that we are setting up the knowledge of the content of the Bible as a goal in and of itself. As we said at the outset, the Bible may or may not be the word of God to persons today. And simply to know its content does not by any means guarantee that it will be the word of God to any person. On the other hand, it should be abundantly clear that if one has no notion of what it says, there is no possibility that it will be the word of God to him. And so we are proposing that we help our children and our boys and girls to study the Bible in such a fashion that they will understand what it says. This presupposes that all the persons involved in the study—those who serve as teachers as well as those who are pupils—recognize the Bible as a book of enough importance to warrant the painstaking study which is required for its understanding.

Boys and girls are not likely to have this attitude just by being told that the Bible is important, that they should study it. No, they will develop this attitude only through their own experience. If, from the time they have been little children, they have been associated with persons who really use the Bible and who really find in it comfort and courage and insight, if their earliest personal contact with the Bible through stories and poems and verses has given them the experience of finding for themselves that the Bible is interesting—that it is a *good* book, in reality as well as in words—then they will wish to know more about it, to understand more completely its teachings. And so we shall, from the beginning, recognize that the Bible can be the word of God to men only as it enters into the experiences of men; we shall use the Bible to throw light upon present experience, to illuminate the meaning of present trials and joys. If it re ains merely the record of God's dealings with men of Bible lands in the long ago, it may be interesting but it will not transform life. Only as it reenters present life can it change life.

We shall, then, begin with life and find in the Bible guidance for life. But we shall recognize also that there must be opportunity for persons to lift up their eyes unto the hills as well as to find light upon their path. They must know something of the experience of others which is deeper, more profound than their own experience. And so we shall not limit our use of the Bible to those passages which afford immediate help in present experience. We shall also provide opportunity, as the children increase in wisdom and in stature, for them to explore more fully the Bible record. And if this exploration is undertaken in companionship with more experienced persons who, in their turn, seek help from books, conferences, and personal study, we may with confidence expect that growing boys and girls will find it richly rewarding. Not because someone else told them, not because it is so written in the creed of their church, but out of their own experience they will come to know that the Bible is the word of God.

XI

The Church and Children

IN CHRISTIAN FAMILIES LITTLE CHILDREN ARE EARLY introduced to the church. The little children's group at the church is among the very first "outside-the-home" relationships such children establish. Likewise, many families which lay no claim to being Christian wish their children to go to church. And if their experiences there are happy, if they feel that it is a friendly place where persons are kind and thoughtful of little children and where there are other little children, it is likely that they will enjoy going to church. Indeed, a nursery or kindergarten class has to be pretty *bad* before little children become reluctant to go.

As they grow older and have wider experience with other institutions, boys and girls are likely to make comparisons. Sometimes they do not find the church program as interesting as they find club activities; and if baseball games or swimming or skating are planned by some group for Sunday, they raise questions regarding their own church attendance. Parents ask themselves, "Just how important *is* it really? Is it important enough for us to insist that the children go?" The answer depends partly upon what happens when the children get to church, and it depends also upon the parents' view of the significance of the church and what it ought to be.

Meeting at Madras, India, in December, 1938, the International Missionary Council confessed the sins of the church as a whole in these words:

In the presence of . . . . disasters and forbodings, we see the judgment of God's righteousness upon our society; but we see also his judgment upon our churches—so enmeshed in the world that they dare not speak God's full word of truth unafraid, so divided that they cannot speak that word with full power, so sullied by pettiness and worldliness that the face of Christ cannot be clearly discerned in them, or his power go forth through them for redemption.

The Significance of the Church

In spite of all these difficulties and these serious limitations, does the church merit loyalty? Does it offer to men and women, to children and growing boys and girls something which no other institution offers or can offer? Is the church *essential?*

The Madras Conference, after making its confession, makes this confident assertion: "Yet in all humility and penitence, we are constrained to declare to a baffled and needy world that the Christian Church under God, is its greatest hope."

Historically, the influence of the church has been described in outline thus:

The earliest church was an informal fellowship, without buildings or ceremonies but bound together by a profound loyalty to Jesus Christ. The persons who gathered in his name, in spite of persecution, became "living cells within the dying organism of an empire, a culture, a civilization."

The church of the years before the fall of Rome was "the one institution with sufficient inherent vitality and tenacity to survive the catastrophic disintegration of a whole civilization."

The church of the middle ages was the "center of all life, guardian of learning, of education, of philanthropy, of medicine, of justice, of faith."

The church of the Reformation again rescued "spiritual

134

reality and freedom from the strangling grip of dry rot, this time the death-hand of a corrupt ecclesiastical hierarchy—proclaiming afresh an ideal for every soul."

The church of the nineteenth century was the "most fertile and fruitful in the long sequence, fountainsource of the most notable succession of crusades for mankind's liberation and relief in history—for abolition of the slave trade, prison reform, ... improved conditions of labor, equality for women, elimination of child labor, temperance, world peace."

And the church of today is "the single unshattered community of all peoples in a world racked with conflict and threatened with death." [1]

Such achievements are notable for any institution in history, and they demand respect. But this is not all that is claimed for the church. It is more than the *best* among the institutions of mankind. It is more than an institution which has had a tremendous influence upon men and upon the course of history. It is unique. It is the *body of Christ*, the channel in today's world through which the purposes of God are kept continuously in contact with men, challenging them, inspiring them, encouraging them. It is "the household of God, the family in which the fatherhood of God and the brotherhood of man is to be realized in the children of his adoption." [2]

"Let the church be the church!" says the report of the great Oxford Conference on Christian Life and Work. Let the church be a unique institution, one which declares the word of God, which challenges contemporary life in the name of God, which acknowledges allegiance to no ruler save God only. "Let the Church be a habitation for God

---

[1] H. P. Van Dusen, *Reality and Religion*, Association Press, 1939, pp. 65-66.

[2] From the report of the Edinburgh Conference on Faith and Order, 1937.

—a community of Christians where God may dwell and make manifest his Kingdom and power and glory. Let the church be a habitation for God, not merely another socially minded institution." [3]

The Unique Character of the Church

These are high claims and high demands. If they are justified, then the church *does* have a unique place, and participation in the life of the church *is* important.

Are they justified; or is the church today, as some among us say, merely one human institution among many, where persons of similar social background get together for social experience and participation in more or less beautiful and meaningful ceremonies of a religious nature? It is important that we arrive at a clear conviction on this basic matter of the significance of the church. We have no right to educate our children within an institution if that institution has become impotent and is destined to die; we have no right to call upon them to give their loyalty to an institution that is not worthy of it. On the other hand, if the church is worthy of their loyalty above that to any other institution, if it does have a unique and all-important function in redeeming men, then we are under obligation to interpret it to them in a manner far more compelling than our present efforts.

Through fellowship in the church persons have the support of others who share their purposes, their joys and sorrows, their aspirations and feelings of frustration. And they have more. They have, in the community of believers in Christ, the experience of Christ. Dr. C. C. Morrison interprets the call of Paul on the road to Damascus as an experience of Christ through experience with the Christian

---

[3] E. F. Tittle, "Let the Church Be the Church," in *Theology and Modern Life*, Willett, Clark, 1940, p. 271.

community. Paul had been persecuting the Christian community. Then he was confronted with Christ—not, Dr. Morrison says, an "absentee Christ," but "the Christ who was alive in the body of his church, who identified himself, in response to Saul's question, as the One Saul was persecuting." [4]

In persecuting the members of the Christian community Paul was persecuting Christ, because Christ was *in* the Christian community; it was his body.

The unique character of the church is not due to magical powers that have been conferred upon it nor to the perfection of its members. The church may refuse to be the church, and sometimes does. When it so refuses it is not the body of Christ but an association of persons for various purposes. It has sometimes stood against the rights of men and for the special privileges of the few; it has sometimes well-nigh forgotten God in its enthusiasm for good works; it has sometimes become merely the carrier of religious ceremonials from generation to generation. But God yearns over the sinful church as he yearns over sinful persons and will not let it go. "I will heal their backsliding" was spoken of Israel, the religious community. The church has survived, alike, persecution and great power and wealth because it carries the germ of life: faith in God.

Paul knew that the members of the churches he had established were not perfect, and he called them to repent and to reform. But in spite of this, he saw the Christian community as the one hope of interpreting the mind of Christ, of testifying to the reality and power of God, and of embodying the will of God before men. The present-day church, too, is made up of persons, human beings, who sin and repent, fail and try again. But in spite of this, it is

---

[4] *What Is Christianity?* Willett, Clark, 1940, p. 154.

the one institution which calls men to God. It is, then, our responsibility as teachers of children and boys and girls to exalt the church and at the same time to strive to bring the church-that-is into harmony with the church-that-ought-to-be.

The church-that-ought-to-be will likely not be a popular church. Yet, it will not be apart from the world; it will be *in* the world, seeking to bring the world to God. It will carry on the work of Jesus. As the work of Jesus was in conflict with the popular thought both of religion and of morality, so the church today will, probably, bear in its body the marks of suffering, because it will be in conflict with the world.

Should the church, then, be a restricted membership of persons who are wholly dedicated to the will of God as revealed in Jesus Christ? Should it make high demands upon its members and expect only a small minority in the community to accept them? It has been suggested in more than one quarter that the church would be much stronger if it were smaller but more devoted to its mission.

In the end of the day, it may be seen that the churches have been mistaken in encouraging men to continue in nominal affiliation, when they had contentedly relegated religion to a quite minor attention . . . . in rejoicing in the fragments of important men's attention which they were successful in claiming. The apostasy of the churches is . . . . that they acquiesced in the common attitude and accommodated themselves to its acceptance. The power of RELIGION within society is . . . . in the true devotion of those, many or few, who know in their spirits what RELIGION is.[5]

Certainly there can be no doubt that the church in America today is made up of persons to whom religion is

---

[5] Van Dusen, *God in These Times*, pp. 69-70.

a matter of supreme importance and, also, of persons to whom it is a matter, at best, of only marginal importance. The Christians in Corinth, probably the most corrupt city of ancient times, recognized that in accepting the mind of Christ as their own they were setting themselves apart from the world about them, at least so far as their values were concerned. It is at this point that the modern church seems to have fallen short. It has "conformed to this world" rather than saying to its members, "Be ye transformed by the renewing of your mind, that ye may prove what is the good and acceptable and perfect will of God." It seems not to have *expected* its members to be "different"!

The Protestant churches do not have, as do the Roman Catholic churches, any one voice which is for them the authoritative, infallible voice of God. But many inadequacies, we venture to suggest, are due, not to human fallibility in interpreting the will of God, but to lack of concern to know the will of God. If the churches are not exercising the influence they should exercise in the affairs of men and nations today, it is because they have not, in season and out of season, called upon men to seek first the will of God.

The Local Church in Its Relationships

The church as our children first come to know it is a *local* church, a particular fellowship of persons, which meets in a particular building in a particular community. Moreover, this local church is part of a larger group of local churches which is a denomination. And denominations are related more or less closely in several interdenominational organizations, such as the Federal Council of Churches, the International Council of Religious Education, and certain missionary organizations. And, finally, they are, most of them, related to an international organization, the World Council of Churches.

How can we interpret this complicated structure to boys and girls without causing, on the one hand, hopeless confusion, and, on the other, loss of confidence in the Christian Church as the body of Christ? It seems so full of divisions. How can it confront the world with a challenging "Thus saith the Lord"? As has been suggested, the churches are made up of human beings who have limitations. They are not yet perfectly devoted to the will of God, perfectly attuned to the mind of Christ. The ideal for the Church of Christ is not yet realized in the churches. They are in process of becoming what they ought to be. And so we shall not expect perfection. Moreover, we shall point out that, because people are different, some persons prefer one mode of worship or type of building or form of organization, while other persons prefer another. But all are part of the Church Universal.

Boys and girls who are to be really effective members of the Church of Christ in the world cannot harbor irreligious prejudices. There need to be, for all children in America, opportunities for friendly relations with persons whose religious faith is different from their own and opportunities to discuss these differences. Such discussions, if wisely led, will reveal among religious groups which have seemed far apart a surprisingly large area of agreement on such essential matters as the fatherhood of God, the brotherhood of man, and the practical way of life which such beliefs require of all present-day men and women and boys and girls.

We shall succeed or fail in these efforts largely to the degree that in the local community where the child lives his own church and the other churches work together in mutual respect, co-operating to meet community needs. For the child's experience in his own local church will be a prelude for experience with the Church Universal.

Relating Children to the Church

How, then, shall we relate children to the church? What shall we expect of it for them?

In many churches there is some ceremony of dedication for babies. Of course, this ceremony does not have significance to the baby. But it may have significance to the parents. It is a symbol of the parents' recognition of the Church of Christ as a unique institution which may, in a special manner, help "all things belonging to the Spirit" to "live and grow" in the child and "all sinful affections" to die. It is a symbol of the parents' desire and purpose to rear the child within the fellowship of the church.

Parents who have such desires and purposes and expectations will help their children to form favorable attitudes toward the church even before the children have any firsthand experience of the church. Because they have regard for the church, the children will be inclined to have regard for it. Because they give evidence of finding in the church satisfying experiences of fellowship and of corporate worship, the children will be inclined to expect such satisfying experiences. Because they give time and thought and money to the program of the church, the children will be inclined to consider participation in the life and work of the church a normal part of happy living. But if the church is ignored in the family during the child's early years, it will be to him an alien institution, strange and unfamiliar.

When the child begins to attend the sessions planned by his church for him, the influence of the parents becomes more specific. If the parents attend regularly and express appreciation of the services, the child is likely to be sympathetic toward the program of the church and to wish to

141

do his share in its work. Going to church and working in the church is a family project. On the other hand, if the parents are careless in attendance and given to casual, unfriendly criticism, the child is likely to become even more careless and even more critical.

It is important, too, during these early years of participation in the life of the church for the parents and other church workers to help the child feel that he is in a real sense a member of the church family. These persons responsible in a peculiar sense for the children should not be modest in their efforts to keep constantly before the adult membership of the church the needs and the privileges of the children. They should make opportunities for the children to meet, under the most favorable circumstances, the officers of the church, the leaders in the women's organizations, the young people who are taking an active part in the work of the church. Especially, they should provide frequent opportunities for the children to meet the pastor and to become acquainted with him as a friend. And they should strive continually as responsible members of the adult membership to make the church a *good* church, worthy of being the spiritual home of little children.

Moreover, these workers can help the church membership as a whole to recognize the rights of the children to participate in the decisions of the church family regarding plans and programs and expenditures, just so far as the children can understand them. The growing boys and girls may best be prepared for full participation as responsible, active members of the church through actual experience in participation.

There will, of course, be planned for children at each age level the very best program that can be planned, and there will be provided the very best teachers and equipment that can be provided. Detailed suggestions for this program

142

and equipment and teacher education are provided in several excellent books and pamphlets and periodicals, and so will not be considered here.

The Influence of the Local Church Fellowship

Surrounding and supporting this specific program for children is the total fellowship of the church family. Those who are most closely related to the program of the church for the children, the leaders in the specific activities of children, we shall, for the moment, assume to be thoroughly trained and able to measure up to all requirments in their personal relations with the children. Is there anything more that needs to be done to make the situation an excellent one in which religious growth may take place? Before answering this question another must be put: Are these the only persons in the church family who influence the children?

There is the pastor. He is the leader of the church, and, if he is worthy of his position, he has more influence than any other person in determining the quality of the life of the Christian community. What is his attitude toward the children? Does he consider their nurture as one of his major responsibilities and greatest opportunities? Or does he think of the work with children, along with the preparation of the monthly dinner for the board of trustees as a task to be delegated?

A ten-year-old boy who had been in the church school since his nursery days and who was active in the work of the junior department asked the leader one Sunday morning, "Who is that man over there talking to Miss Orr?" The leader looked—and saw the pastor of the church! He had not recently come to the congregation but had been the minister for over a year. And yet here was an alert ten-year-old boy, an enthusiastic member of the church school,

143

who had apparently never before even so much as seen his pastor!

Surely something important is missing from the experience of children in that large and beautifully equipped church. And yet, the evidence seems to indicate that this is no isolated situation among the large city churches. Of course, the minister of such a church is busy. We are not suggesting that he should take the aggressive leadership in children's work. The chances are that neither by training nor inclination is he the best person in the church to do that. But he *is* the pastor of the children in the primary department just as really as he is pastor of the chairman of the Board of Trustees or of the president of the Woman's Missionary Society. As such, he is of necessity a vital factor in the total program of religious education in the church.

Probably the most important need is for the boys and girls to feel that the pastor is a friend. Except in very large churches, he can really know the children if he considers it important.

Some boys were playing ball on a vacant lot one afternoon when a man stopped to watch. During an interval in the play one of the boys asked, "Who is that fellow standing over there?" "Why that's Dr. Rivers!" Joe exclaimed, and hurried over. The two chatted for a moment, and then Joe returned to the game. "Who is Dr. Rivers?" Bob wanted to know. "He's the minister at my church and a friend of mine," Joe answered with pride in his voice. Does that fact, the fact that the minister "is a friend of mine," contribute to the influence of Joe's church in his life?

If the minister visits the children's room frequently, sometimes coming early enough to share in the informal activities which the early comers among the children enjoy so much, he may establish these friendly relations easily. He may help decide where the bowl of jonquils will look best, or whether the new picture which has been given to the juniors will be lovelier in a bronze or in a blue frame. He may help a boy find a good picture of an oriental lamp from one of the books in his study; he may put the star on top of the Christmas tree which the children are trimming in the beginners' room, because he is "tallest."

He may worship with one or another of the children's groups, not necessarily leading the service but sharing in it. On special invitation he may meet with a certain group throughout the session to consider some questions regarding suffering and death with which the teacher feels unable to deal. When the children's groups have under way some especially interesting enterprise, he may keep in touch with its progress and tell other members of the church family about it. When he leads the congregation in prayer, he may mention the work the children are doing. Thus he may show his interest in the children of his church.

The members of the official board of the church, those who have responsibility for the business affairs of the church, are also contributing to, or hindering, the influence of the church upon the lives of its children. And this in spite of the fact that they have little contact with the children. The manner in which the business of the church is conducted, the promptness with which bills are paid, the fairness of the salary paid to the minister and the janitor, the responsibility they feel for keeping the church property in repair—in the handling of such matters, the officers of the church are teaching the children.

The generosity of the church in providing for its children the best possible meeting places and equipment, the friendly interest of all the adults in the activities of the children, their concern for the welfare of the growing life within their fellowship—these evidences of the thought and care of their church draw the child to it in love and gratitude. The actual quality of this provision is not the most important matter. Some churches provide lavish equipment but spend little thought on their children. If it is the best the church can afford, the children will rejoice in it, however modest it may be.

The approach of the church in dealing with differences of opinion among its members, in hearing all sides, in helping persons who differ to understand one another's point of view and to respect it, in seeking to find the solution which is best for all concerned and which can be supported by all —in such approaches to problems in human relations the children learn what it means not to look, each one, to his own interest, but also to the interests of others.

The outreach of the church beyond its own present membership into the community, the courageous and intelligent efforts it puts forth in behalf of those members of the community who are beyond the fellowship of the responsible citizens and who are unhappy, lonely, in need of physical help or of support for their cause in the courts or before the appropriation committee of the city governing body— such activities within the church stimulate the children to wish to share in extending the fellowship of the church to all men.

Thus the church may become a spiritual home for growing boys and girls. It may be for them really a revelation of the will of God operating among men.

Assuming the Vows of Church Membership

At what point in their development should boys and girls be invited to assume the vows of full membership in the church? There can, of course, be no one answer to this question. A great deal depends upon the point of view and the custom of the particular local church to which they are immediately related. In many churches today children are regarded as being *within* the fellowship of the church, as members of the church family, from the time they are first brought into contact with the church. If they are christened or dedicated in some other manner in infancy, or are entered on the roll of the nursery department, they are from that moment a part of the life of the church, and the church assumes a share of the responsibility for their nurture. When they begin to attend the sessions of the church planned for them, they are participating in the life of the church. As they move from one group to another within the church, the ceremony of promotion from one to the next should provide opportunity for interpretation, on the level of the child's understanding, of the meaning of discipleship to Jesus Christ and of the fellowship within the Christian Church, and for opportunity for the child to make his own personal commitment on his own level of understanding.

From the time they are six or seven years of age, children enjoy the opportunity of finding out about the work of their own church and of sharing in it. When they reach the junior department of the church, they will probably be ready to appreciate a simple narrative account of the beginnings and the development of the Christian Church. During this period, too, will likely come some consideration of the nature of the church, of its unity in diversity, of how it differs from other institutions, and what is its place in the present-day world, though there will be reserved until junior-high-school or high-school age detailed, long-term attention to these matters.

Along with appreciation of the unique character and worth of the church must go, as has been suggested, a frank recognition on the part of parents and teachers that the

147

church is not perfect, that it has its weaknesses and that it is not doing all that it should do in the world today. If this acknowledgment comes against a long-term experience of satisfying church relationships, the boys and girls will find it helpful and stimulating rather than depressing. They will see that the church does have a great work to do, that it needs clearer understanding of its unique function, more complete devotion to the will of God, more devoted service to men, and more aggressive determination to overcome evil. They will see that the church needs *them* and all they have to offer of intelligence, devotion, and courage; they will see that they need the church.

Such general preparation over several years will help the child to desire to assume the vows of full membership in the church. But he will need also some special preparation for the actual ceremony. Usually, this preparation will be in the hands of the pastor, working in close cooperation with the children's workers of the church and the parents. He will wish to talk with the boys and girls thoughtfully about the church, to satisfy himself that they are ready to assume the vows of full membership, and to interpret to them in detail the ritual of their church.

Before the time for assumption of the vows, care should be taken that the adults of the congregation are prepared to look forward to it as an occasion of importance, a ceremony of joy as well as of solemn obligation. For example, in the ritual of one church the minister says to the parents:

Let this be to you a day of peculiar joy and thanksgiving, in that these who are of your flesh and blood have also entered into a holier spiritual kinship with you in Jesus Christ.[6]

Similarly, the church family is called upon to rejoice:

---

[6] From *The Ritual of The Methodist Church.* Used by permission of The Methodist Publishing House.

Brethren of the household of faith, let our hearts be lifted up in thanksgiving to Almighty God, who by the Holy Spirit hath inclined these Children to desire and ask for membership in the Church. Having arrived at years of discretion, and now of their own accord appearing before this congregation to take upon themselves the vows and enter upon the privileges and duties of the Church, let us with one mind and heart most earnestly invoke in their behalf the blessings of Father, Son and Holy Spirit.[7]

It cannot be said too emphatically that the service of reception of children into full membership in the church should always be conducted with the utmost dignity. Hurry on the part of the officiating minister, restlessness or inattention on the part of the congregation, will be sensed by the boys and girls and they will be deeply hurt by it. Rather, let the minister give every evidence of his own sense of the profound importance of the occasion, and let the members of the church truly rejoice in it.

The World Christian Community

The child's relationship to the church is, first of all, a relationship to a local church, a fellowship within his own community. The life within that local fellowship and the ritual of reception into full responsibility in it should help clarify for the child (and keep renewing for the total membership) the fact that this local church is not an isolated group but a part of the world community of Christians, the body of Christ, through which the mind of Christ is made known to all the world. As members of this world community, children have privileges and responsibilities beyond those inherent in their participation in the life and work of their own local congregation. They have privileges of world-wide fellowship that transcends barriers of race, class, or nation—even nations at war. And they have re-

[7] *Ibid.*

149

sponsibilities for exerting through it a vital influence for reconciliation among the nations, for healing, for creative activity toward ever-enlarging areas of co-operation, mutual service, and appreciation, making for real world unity.

The concept of world unity is not a new one. In ancient history lie the roots of the idea of a world-wide community which would find its center in the capital of some one people and its source of influence and power in the superior quality of that nation's religion, its citizenship, its manners and customs.

To the patriots of ancient Israel, Jerusalem was to be the center of the world:

> Lift up thine eyes round about, and see: they all gather themselves together, they come to thee; . . . . the abundance of the sea shall be turned unto thee, the wealth of the nations shall come unto thee. . . . . Thy gates also shall be open continually . . . . that men may bring into thee the wealth of the nations, and their kings led captive. For that nation and kingdom that will not serve thee shall perish.

This dream of world unity under the dominance of some one nation has frequently been held before men, and occasionally almost achieved, as under the Roman Empire. In modern times there have been empires which extended over the earth, bringing men of many races under one great system of government, stemming from one capital. But history has demonstrated over and over that this plan of world unity is unsound in its very nature.

The great prophets of Israel spiritualized the concept by lifting Israel from the plane of merely a mighty power to that of a holy nation, whose mission was to bring peace and healing and the knowledge of Jehovah to the earth, so that Israel, the religious community, rather than Israel, the nation, would become the source of world unity.

150

Though it was world unity *under* the chosen people, according to the customs and mores of the Israelites, this thought of unity through loyalty to one God started mankind in a new direction.

It was generations later before the thought of the prophets found its development in Paul's great statement: "There can be neither Jew nor Greek, there can be neither bond nor free, there can be no male and female; for ye all are one man in Christ Jesus." More generations passed while men were slowly and painfully learning the meaning of true world community in Jesus Christ. Even today only a small minority of those who name the name of Christ think of themselves as members of a fellowship which transcends all lines of race, class, and nation. Yet such a fellowship is the Christian Church, the body of Christ. It acknowledges one God as Father; it embraces all men as brothers; it sets its purposes toward doing the will of God and recognizes that world healing can come only as men are made aware of their selfishness and accept the salvation from sin which is offered in the gospel of Jesus Christ.

This fellowship must be more than a dream of the prophets. It must be real among men today. It may grow slowly, but it is growing. Just on the eve of the catastrophe of World War II there were held four gatherings of Christians from all the nations: those at Oxford and at Edinburgh in 1937, at Madras in 1938, and at Amsterdam in 1939. In these meetings were made explicit the unity of Christians around the world. In spite of wide differences of national custom and speech and government, in spite of all shades of opinion on doctrines and church polity, they found that they were one in their faith in God, in the brotherhood of man, in the possibility of salvation from sin, and in their sense of dependence upon God.

The Christian community, beginning as a minority within each nation, but preaching and living its faith, will grow as the mustard seed and will become the hope of the nations for world redemption.

If the child's experience in his own local church and his assumption of the vows of full membership have been full of joy and growing appreciation of the nature and mission of the church in the world today, he is ready also to understand that he is not only a part of his local church but a part of the fellowship of believers that transcends race, class, or nation—the body of Christ. He will feel that the church demands loyalty above other institutions because it is, at once, a channel through which God makes his will known to men and a fellowship of persons who are helping and supporting one another in their commitment to the will of God.

To glorify God and to help men; to proclaim the kingship of God in the earth and to win men in loyalty to it; to be apart from the world in its standards of values and yet to be in the world as an instrument of God in the service and in the salvation of all men—this is the mission of the church in which we invite our children to participate.

XII

Worshiping God

THAT THE GOD OF THE UNIVERSE, WHOSE GREATNESS is unsearchable, the Holy One, the righteous Judge of the earth, also is aware of individual men and seeks fellowship with even the least of these—this is one of the greatest affirmations of Christian faith. To know that the God who created the heavens and the earth, who "weighed the mountains in scales, and the hills in a balance," cares for men, one by one, must seem to men today as wonderful as it seemed to the ancient psalmist.

How shall we help our children to become increasingly aware of God, to find fellowship with God, to understand the language in which God speaks to them, to respond to God? To suggest some approaches to these questions has been the chief concern of the preceding chapters. But it seems well, now, to bring our thoughts to focus on specific questions relating directly to the child's worship.

Acknowledging the Reality and Greatness of God

To normal men confronted by God there comes a sense of awe and humility. One feels compelled to acknowledge God as *God*. "O Lord my God, thou art very great." The experiences recorded in the literature of religion show that noble souls of all the ages who felt themselves in the presence of God have this in common: they recognized their own littleness and the greatness of God.

Little children, feeling wonder in the presence of some miracle of nature, may be led to acknowledge God. This need not be in formal words or even in words at all. It may, and probably will be, an inarticulate response to the mystery they sense. With increasing experience the awareness of God may be deepened by increasing opportunity to "be still, and know that I am God." In these moments of apprehension of God there is no thought of one's own personal need; there is an encompassing sense of the reality and the majesty of God. The response to such experience, however expressed, will reflect the reverence of the Old Testament writers: "Holy, holy, holy, is the Lord of hosts: the whole earth is full of his glory"; "What is man, that thou art mindful of him?"

It seems to be the testimony of the saints throughout the ages that unless one is *aware* of God, unless one acknowledges God as *God*, there is little likelihood of there being an experience of what we call worship. For worship assumes a relationship between God and man, based, on man's side, upon his acknowledgment of the greatness of God.

But this is not all. Man does not merely stand in reverent awe in the presence of God. In worship there is communication. God enters man's experience; he reveals his concern and his purposes, not for men in general, but for each man in particular. The visions of the great mystics are outstanding examples of this experience of communication. But the great mystics themselves disparage the phenomena of sights and sounds as mere adjuncts. The *real* aspect of the experience is the conviction of the presence of God.

There seems little ground for doubt that one may grow in his sensitiveness to the communications of God. There is abundant testimony to the effect that "practicing the presence of God" may increase one's awareness of God and may increase one's ability to understand the language in which he speaks to men.

154

Understanding the Language in Which God Speaks

How may we help our children to grow in sensitiveness to God's presence, in ability to understand the language in which God speaks to us? Professor Calhoun makes these suggestions:

One may hope by patient deciphering of the laws of nature and of human life to discover what details may be discernible of God's will as revealed through the media of actual events. To such interpretation both the acumen of scientists, the vision of poets, the vigor of men of action, and the patient fortitude of plain folk must all contribute. To this end we read our Scriptures and our newspapers, we search the stars and the shop and street-corner, with what wisdom we may. And as we search, the air may brighten and the heart lift from time to time, and we go on, still groping but of good cheer.[1]

That is, we are likely to come to understand the language in which God speaks to us, not primarily in some striking experience, but primarily in the affairs of common life, viewed in the light of all the human wisdom and experience that is available. But there must be opportunity for God to speak. In the midst of the affairs of life there must be pauses in activity in order that the activity may be seen in perspective. "The World is too much with us"; we need to withdraw from it for a moment in order to evaluate it. In such moments of quiet reflection, when the thoughts are directed, not toward the next job to be done, but toward God and his purposes for us, there is likely to come fresh insight into a problem, a thought of a new approach to a person who has been unresponsive; a suggestion of something to do to relieve a difficult situation; a reminder of selfish and unco-operative attitudes and behavior on one's own part, requiring correction.

If, following the very best insight which we gain, the

---

[1] *God and the Common Life,* p. 243.

clearest understanding that has come to us, we go back into our activities and use this insight and understanding, we may expect that our insight and our understanding will grow. But if we refuse it, if we go on our own way without regard to it, then we may not expect to increase in our ability to understand the voice of God when he speaks to us. It is of the very first importance that we help our children to apprehend this truth. "No angel visitant, no opening skies" are likely to appear to them; yet God speaks! In the simple everyday opportunities that are afforded he speaks, and only as our hearts are attuned to these promptings of the spirit of God may we grow in understanding of his language.

Fellowship with God Through Doing His Will

Again, if we believe that God is working in our world, it behooves us to find him there and to align ourselves with his purposes. In the effort to further God's purposes, man will become aware of a sense of fellowship with God. Indeed, the great prophets announced that only through cooperation in the purposes of God could fellowship with God be realized. Not through ceremonies, sacrifices, or even prayers, they said, but through honesty and justice and mercy and service to the needy would one find fellowship with God.

I hate, I despise your feasts, and I will take no delight in your solemn assemblies. . . . . Take thou away from me the noise of thy songs. . . . . But let justice roll down as waters, and righteousness as a mighty stream.

Your new moons and your appointed feasts my soul hateth; they are a trouble unto me; I am weary of bearing them. And when ye spread forth your hands, I will hide mine eyes from you; yea, when ye make many prayers, I will not hear. . . . . Wash you, make you clean; put away the evil of your doings from before mine eyes; cease to do evil; learn to do well; seek justice, relieve the oppressed, judge the fatherless, plead for the widow.

In such flashing words the prophets of the righteousness of God called his children to do away with the signs and symbols and words of worship, and approach God directly through doing his will: righting wrongs, showing mercy, extending kindness. The importance for our children of this interpretation today has already been pointed out. It requires a careful scrutiny of all our teachings, of the ceremonies, the services we plan, of the materials we use. It is true that sometimes religious observances have been made "an opiate" dulling the sense of unrighteousness rather than a nourishing food developing insight and courage. In present-day churches as well as among the ancient Israelites the form of religion has sometimes been substituted for its reality.

It must be assumed, then, that only as men recognize the reality of God, listen to the voice of God, and seek to carry out his purposes in all their human relationships will they find a vital and glowing sense of fellowship with God. But we know, too, that one does not *first* recognize the reality of God and *then* hear him speak and *then* do his will by loving and serving one's fellowmen and *then* come to have fellowship with God. These experiences do not follow in any such sequence. In fact, they do not follow in any sequence at all. Rather, each contributes to, and grows stronger through, the other. One's sense of the reality of God is strengthened by participation in the life of other persons, and experiences of communion with God increase one's desire to serve one's fellows. One cannot merely *will* to have a sense of the reality of God, or fellowship with him, and be sure that it will follow. But one may do those things which he conceives to be the will of God, and

157

one may put himself in those situations where it seems reasonable to expect God's purposes to be realized.

Beautiful stories in literature portray the finding of God, not in romantic searches for the Holy Grail in distant lands, but in simple acts of human kindness near at home; not in pilgrimages to Jerusalem, but in service to humble folk along the way; not in keeping the sacred flame in burnished lamps upon high altars, but in using its warmth to comfort shivering children. Many men and women whose lives have never been perpetuated in literature testify to the truth in these stories: one does not find God by concentrating on the search for him but by acting always as if one knew he was near. We may remind our children of the saying of Jesus, "Inasmuch as ye did it unto one of these my brethren, even these least, ye did it unto me," and encourage in them the faith that in such ways as these they are most likely to experience for themselves a sense of the reality of God.

Prayer and the Sense of the Reality of God

There is need also for the specific expression of one's sense of the reality of God and of his communication with men. The very attempt to give expression to one's thoughts of God, to one's desires to do the will of God, helps to clarify one's thinking. Feelings after God sometimes fail to come to any satisfying experience because one leaves them in a state of diffused, nebulous vagueness rather than attempting to bring them to focus. In expressing one's aspirations they become more clear and appear more attainable; one sees where there is need for additional thought and where there is need for immediate action upon the insight one already has.

The most usual form of expression for one's yearning after God is through prayer. Very little children talk things over with their parents, and, if it is suggested to them, they come to talk things over with God in much the same informal fashion.

Among the first prayers of little children will be expressions of joy in the beauty of the earth and in the satisfactions of normal needs. These will not in all likelihood be phrased as prayers at all but will be spontaneous outpourings of praise. "I love you, world!" a little girl exulted, stretching out her arms to the sunshine and wind and trees. As he grows, parents and teachers may guide the child in conscious experiences and expressions of gratitude and thanksgiving. They will also help him to find satisfaction in asking God to help him to think of others, to plan for their happiness. And when things have gone wrong, they will direct his thoughts to God, asking help in finding better ways of playing and working with others. Thus God becomes increasingly real to the little child.

As his experiences broaden there will be an increasing field for prayer. Parents and teachers may help the growing boy and girl to direct attention to those phases of experience in which there is special need for the help of God. For forgiveness when one has put his own above his neighbor's welfare, for insight that one may discern good from evil in a complex civilization, for strength to do the best we know in every situation—for all such matters we know God wants us to pray, and we know God will help us.

Prayer for Self-centered Ends

Unfortunately, there appear to remain, even among adults, strange and unchristian conceptions and practices of prayer, so that, instead of being a channel of communication between God and man, it becomes, actually, a stumbling block in the way of one's apprehending the purposes of God. Amazing as it may seem, there is abundant evidence that countless mature persons today hold a view of prayer which makes it a means of *getting what they want.* They speak piously of their "faith in prayer," when what they really mean is that they propose to use prayer as a key to unlock all the barriers that stand between them and the things or the positions they want. It is a sort of magic which they use to compel the forces of the universe to do their bidding. They appear to think that if they just pray long enough and loudly enough they can assault the gates of heaven, so to speak, and lay hold on the power of God for their own purposes.

Jesus repudiated such thoughts of prayer. In the story of the temptation he specifically refused to make any demands upon God. Suggestions that he appropriate the power of God for the satisfaction of his own physical needs, that he call for bands of angels to demonstrate the favor of God, that he assume authority over lands and persons—these suggestions he turned aside with the positive statement: "Get thee hence, Satan." It seems clear that many prayers in Christian groups are more nearly in harmony with the suggestions which Jesus repudiated as the suggestions of Satan than in harmony with the purposes of God as Jesus revealed them to us. They are self-centered, presumptuous, demanding. And prayers in this spirit are destructive in their effects upon the person praying.

No one human being may assume the right to tell another what are and what are not "suitable" subjects of prayer. God knows us altogether; he knows all our thoughts, our desires, our aspirations. To say that one must not pray about any subject is foolish because if one deeply desires it, it is, in a sense, already a prayer. We shall not, then, guide our children's prayers by rules of propriety. So long as a child wants to pray for rabbits and footballs and dollhouses and personal success and recognition, for just so long we shall know that his thoughts of God are very limited.

And when the prayers go beyond these limitations and become prayers for vengeance, calling for punishments of those who are unfriendly toward his own cause or his own group or person, we shall know that the child is really praying to a false god, not to the God whom Jesus revealed to men; and we shall seek to help that child clarify his thoughts of God.

Generally it is more satisfactory to approach the problem through positive suggestion rather than through negative reproof. Instead of saying, "It is not good to ask God for a rabbit," it is likely to be more helpful to say, "Shall we talk to God about all his good plans for us?" And then if guidance is offered in the form of a simply worded prayer of gratitude for some happy experience, or for help in knowing what God wants his children to do in a concrete, immediate situation to make someone else happy, the child's thought may be given direction. By helping the child to word his prayers, we may guide the thoughts of his prayers. We may pray *with* him. We may talk over with him what he wishes to say to God or ask God and then word the prayer for him.

There will be, of course, occasions when direct interpretation is needed. When children ask, "Will God do anything I ask him to do?" there should follow a thoughtful conversation, which helps the child to understand that God does not always do what we ask him to do because we often ask him to do things which are not good for us or which are not good for other people. God always does what is *good* for us, even when we do not know that it is good. Many illustrations from actual experience are available to any parent or teacher which will make it abundantly clear to a little child that just as loving parents do not give a child something he wants if that something is harmful, so God who is wise and good does not cease being wise and good

161

just in order to let a child have something he thinks he wants.

It is quite important that this be made very clear to little children while they are little children so that the interpretation may grow as their experience deepens. In the life of almost every person there will come a time when it seems as if he *must* make demands upon God, as if he cannot bear what is before him. Even to Jesus there came such an experience, and he cried, "My God, My God, why hast thou forsaken me?" But if such an experience comes against a background of having learned to trust God, it will likely become clarified. "Father, into thy hands I commend my spirit" will follow the cry of despair. But if such an experience comes against a background of vague notions of prayer as a means of protecting oneself from suffering through appeal to the love of God, it may well be disastrous to a vital faith.

By thinking of Jesus, boys and girls may know that God is deeply concerned about their longings, that he is aware of their sufferings and shares their pain, that he wants them to bring to him every problem and every sorrow. In the fellowship of God they may find comfort and courage even when the cup "cannot pass away."

Prayer for Great Causes

But many persons pray, not for personal relief or comfort or success or favor, but for some cause that is both good and great. To the very best of one's ability to understand, this cause does represent the will of God! Its success will promote the purposes of God; its failure will set back the purposes of God. Surely, for such a great cause—a plan for world peace, a program of social reform that will bring relief to millions of suffering children—surely for such a cause one may pray in full expectation that one's prayer will be answered. Yet often these prayers appear to go unanswered.

On one occasion when his disciples made a request of Jesus, he said to them, "Ye know not what ye ask." In this saying we may see the answer to much of our perplexity about prayers which we think are unanswered. We pray for what to us are *good* ends. But the limits of our knowledge are so narrow! We smile today at the superstitions of backward tribes. Their faith in amulets seems to us pathetic. And yet when we compare our own field of knowledge with that of some outstanding person whom we know or whose works we have read, we are struck with *our* startling ignorance. There are so many fields in which we know nothing at all. The great astronomers, who speak confidently of the laws governing the movements of the plants and of solar systems, the physicists who talk of the unceasing activity of electrons, the geologists who discuss the rigidity and flux of the earth—in the presence of these men we feel keenly the narrow limits of our knowledge. Yet these great men acknowledge that, even in their own specialized field, there are whole areas about which they have no knowledge at all, and so we begin to catch a glimpse of the vast regions beyond the limits of human knowledge.

How, then, in our ignorance of the great, universal purpose of God can we make demands that our interpretation of good be made to prevail? How can we know that it will not interfere with the coming of some greater good? Only if our knowledge were infinite and our purposes were wholly without taint of self could we pray with confidence that what we asked was altogether right. But what would our requests be under these circumstances? Perfect wisdom, perfect goodness—that is God. If we are willing to leave our longings in the hands of God, trusting his wisdom and

163

his love, then we know that our prayers are always answered—not that the result we foresaw will necessarily come to pass, but that *good* results will come to pass.

Shall we say, then, that to pray is, after all, futile? That no purpose is served by attempting to formulate our own best thoughts of a wise approach to a wrong that needs righting or a good that needs doing? By no means.

Because even *one man* prays sincerely for world peace, peace is nearer than it was before he prayed. Prayer is creative; the man who prays sincerely for the triumph of some noble cause is, himself, a changed man. He is better prepared to work for peace; he has new insights, fresh courage, renewed commitment. And so, though the final end is not in view, progress has been made.

In somewhat the same manner as conversation with a wise and trustworthy friend, prayer in itself is good because it provides an opportunity for reviewing, in the consciousness of God's presence, all one's activities and plans and thus coming to see them in truer perspective.

God can do through men who pray what he cannot do through men who do not pray, because the man who prays comes increasingly to understand the purposes of God and renews his strength to undertake the hard, often unpopular work that must be done to realize those purposes in the earth. And so men pray, not to persuade a reluctant God to do some good which he is not ready to do, but to make it possible for God to use them to do the good which he is purposing. They pray in faith, trusting implicitly the love and wisdom of God. Such men *do* make a difference in the progress of good causes in the earth. For the man who really prays in faith, who truly seeks to know the will of God that he may do it, goes out from his prayer also to work in faith. The insight gained from the prayer enables him to work more effectively, more confidently, and

164

the work, in turn, clarifies the problems about which he has prayed and so sends him back to prayer with new needs and fresh hopes. Thus man learns to know God and to have fellowship with him.

Our children may, then, be encouraged to pray for causes and to feel that their prayer accomplishes something.

Prayer for Others

Our children also may be encouraged to pray for others in full assurance that their prayers do make a difference. When someone is in sorrow or perplexity or has sinned, the prayers of those who love him bring about a new situation. Outgoing love and concern are positive and real forces. They change the direction of the lives of persons. When this love and concern for one's neighbor is dedicated to God, it is used of him in ways which we need not understand in order to accept. The evidence is clear and abundant.

When someone is sick, the prayers of those who love him do not change God's intentions; they do not recall God to some good which has been neglected; but, rather, they release resources of healing which were not available before the person prayed. These resources become a real factor in recovery. And if recovery is not possible, they are resources of comfort and courage.

Such prayers for others also change the person who prays. He is willing to be used of God to help the one for whom he has prayed. He has more insight into the needs of that person and into ways in which he may meet those needs. He is in very truth a channel through which the resources of God are brought to bear upon the lives of those about him.

Perhaps there should be suggested a caution lest we develop a self-conscious sense of mission in our children which

165

will be harmful both to them and to others. A humble, sincere sense of mission, of being used of God, is wholesome and profoundly Christian. But anything that savors of spiritual pride, of presumptuous claim to special insight, is much more likely to be evidence, again, of the promptings of Satan than of the spirit of God.

Through actual experience in prayer with sympathetic, understanding adults, children may gradually move beyond the point where they will think of prayer as primarily "asking God," or "telling God," to the point where they will think of prayer primarily in the spirit of Jesus, as seeking to know the will of God, of finding in prayer true fellowship with God. We need not expect our children to be precocious here any more than in other areas of development, but we may expect them to *grow*.

Using Worship Materials

To many seeking souls there seems to be need for something more than encouragement to pray. Their worship seems fruitless, cold, meaningless. To such persons the resources of religious literature, the expressions of the faith and aspirations of great souls to whom God was very real, have often been helpful in bringing their own pale faith to a brighter glow; the singing of the words of a glorious hymn of praise has helped to stimulate their own sluggard spirits; the participation in a noble litany, wrought out of the dedication of consecrated lives, has lifted their own weak zeal to high endeavor.

There are such materials suitable for use with children. There are materials, prepared especially for children of various ages, which may clarify the child's thought of worship. As Jesus gave his disciples a suggested form of prayer to help them understand the meaning of prayer, so we may often help our children, not so much by discussing worship with them as by sharing with them the experience of using the language of worship of some person whose insights and faith exceed our own.

Of course merely to "say words," no matter how beautiful they may be or how rich in association with the saints of the ages, is not to worship God. The child must be able to enter into the spirit of the words and make them his own. He does not need to understand every word or the turn of every phrase. But the whole intent and purpose of the prayer or litany he must understand if it is to be really his own language of worship. Some conversation about it will usually remove any serious difficulties in understanding and will also help to direct the attention of the boys and girls specifically to the thoughts and aspirations being expressed.

Unfortunately, a great many of the religious songs in modern times have been astonishingly bad music, bad literature, and bad theology. The greatest care should be given to the words of songs used in worship, as these words are influential in directing the child's thoughts of God and of social relationships. But there are available excellent sources of really good songs for use with children—songs which offer words expressing worthy aspirations in beautiful and meaningful literary form, and set to worthy music that is within the range of children's voices. Through such songs boys and girls may find a satisfying expression of their desire to worship.

Great poetry expressing faith in God and in man's status as a child of God may afford both stimulating and comforting resources in Christian devotions. And in the Bible there is the greatest wealth of materials, reflecting the experience of men and women through the ages to whom God was very near and very real. To use this material as a language of worship requires, of course, that we select those portions which may reasonably be expected to stimulate the child's aspirations and give them meaningful expression. Some selections, saturated in figures of speech which they cannot yet interpret, will be confusing rather than helpful. For example, we should avoid such passages as this:

The Lord is my rock, and my fortress, and my deliverer, even mine;
God, my rock, in him will I take refuge;
My shield, and the horn of my salvation, my high tower, and my refuge.

Though it represents a splendid piling up of figures to express confidence in God, it is confusing to children.

On the other hand, boys and girls can come increasingly to love and find satisfaction in this simple poem of joy in God's love and care:

Make a joyful noise unto the Lord, all ye lands.
Serve the Lord with gladness:
Come before his presence with singing.
Know ye that the Lord, he is God:
It is he that hath made us, and we are his;
We are his people, and the sheep of his pasture.
Enter into his gates with thanksgiving,
And into his courts with praise:
Give thanks unto him, and bless his name.
For the Lord is good; his lovingkindness endureth forever,
And his faithfulness into all generations.

Some of these materials we shall encourage the children to memorize. Merely to be able to say the words will not be especially valuable, but if boys and girls use the materials frequently and come to associate them with their own experiences, the materials will become more and more significant. And because they know them they can use them freely in group worship both at home and in the church.

Using the Literature of the Church

The liturgical churches stress the significance of materials of worship which have been tested in the experience of the race, and of sacraments and ceremonials which have gathered to themselves rich associations and meanings. They feel that boys and girls should early be introduced to these materials. They consider the very fact that the expressions and the ceremonies have come from great souls through the years gives them value above other materials for present-day boys and girls and that, in using them, present-day worshipers may share the experience out of which they came.

Other persons feel that the thought of the unity of the Christian community in all lands is enriched through the use of this common material and that, therefore, children should come to know it while they are yet children.

Thus to hear the aspirations and affirmations of faith of the church as they have been recorded in literature and symbols and sacraments helps growing persons, of whatever age, to feel that they, too, may aspire unto them. Our children need material that helps them to lift up their eyes unto the hills, as well as material that throws light upon their immediate path. To catch a glimpse of spiritual life, at present beyond them, but beautiful and appealing, is as helpful and as needful to children as is specific guidance in daily living.

All these values are real and should be conserved. It should always be remembered, however, that to teach a child a prayer or a hymn or a litany or to introduce him to a symbol or a sacrament before there is in his own experience a real basis for appreciating its meaning may easily

169

hinder rather than help him. If he becomes involved in confusing and symbolic language, he is not likely to find in that language or those symbols help in clarifying and enriching his thoughts of God or his experience of God. Our purpose, then, should be to consider, on the one hand, the experiences and the readiness of the boys and girls, and, on the other, the great and beautiful expressions of the faith of the church. At the points, and to the extent, that the materials may be made meaningful to children we shall use them in deep gratitude and appreciation.

Group Worship

To many persons a sense of the reality of God and fellowship with him comes most readily through group worship. Indeed, there are some thoughtful students who are of the opinion that it is primarily when persons feel themselves a part of a group, responsible for, and responsive to, others, that they are likely to have a real experience of God. Togetherness among human personalities is, beyond doubt, a great incentive to the worship of God. We are "members one of another," as the New Testament declares. We become persons only in association with other persons, and awareness of ourselves as persons among other persons increases both the capacity and the desire for fellowship with the great "other Person" in the universe.

In the home and in the church boys and girls need the experience of group worship. When life in a home characterized by sincere devotion on the part of each member to the happiness and welfare of the others is supported by family fellowship in the worship of God, a child has a source of security and of insight into the meaning of life which can scarcely be overestimated. When he participates in group worship of God which is Christian in its spirit and its purpose, he learns more about the meaning of worship

170

than he could ever learn through direct teaching. In such a situation life with God is more than a phrase; it is real.

In the church children need the experience of worshiping with others of their own age. Through carefully selected materials the leaders of the group can help children at each level of their development to nobler concepts of God and to a more vital sense of fellowship with him. Singing together and praying together, working together and playing together in the children's departments of the church provide opportunities for little children to begin to understand that they are a part of the great family of God. In such a group with a competent leader the children have an opportunity to learn what loving one another and preferring one another means when one is living, not with his own family where he has a "special" place, but with a group of his peers, all of whom feel that they have "special" places! They learn that there are many different persons in God's family and that each one is important to God and may talk to God.

As a child grows older and learns more of the great hymns of the church, comes to appreciate larger portions of the Bible, responds to litanies and partakes of sacraments, he begins to sense the power of corporate worship really to make a difference in his outlook and his way of behaving. In his own group in the church the materials are carefully chosen so that they may be his own language of worship, and the services are not too heavy nor too long. Thus he is experiencing the values of corporate worship on his own level. He is strengthening his own present faith through the support of the faith of those about him. And he is laying a sound foundation for a growing faith as he becomes ready to participate in the corporate worship of the congregation.

Participating in the Corporate Worship of the Church

At just what age a child will be invited to participate in the worship of the entire congregation will depend upon the child's own development, the customs of the denomination of which his church is a part, and the particular emphases of his own parents, teachers, and minister. There was a time when all the children above the age of two or three were taken to the church service—and sometimes the babies as well. Now there is general agreement that little children who find it impossible to sit comfortably on church pews or to participate in the service not only fail to receive spiritual help, but distract the attention of the adults near them. And so there is agreement that it is better to leave these little children at home, or in the church nursery if one is provided. But when children begin to go to school, some parents and ministers feel that they should attend the service of worship of the congregation, and many more parents and ministers feel that boys and girls of junior age and above should attend.

A prior question should be asked before asking at what age a child should attend the church service. It is this: What is it expected that the congregational worship service will provide which is not provided in the remaining parts of the church program for this age group? The long and difficult road that has been traveled to secure a graded program for the children of the church has brought us to the place where we have an almost separate church life for each age group. Because this graded program is necessary, there is hesitation on the part of children's leaders to take any steps which will seem to render it unnecessary. They know that beginners' songs and adult hymns are as far apart as are the children's bedtime stories and the books of Thomas Hardy, and that this must be so if there is to be provided a suitable language of worship for each group. They know

172

that juniors need to think through problems of social relationships apart from the adults who have already settled them for themselves. They know that young people need the opportunity to consider the ethics of the present economic order as tested by the principles of Jesus, unhindered on the one hand by the presence of little children who have too little data to take part in the discussions, and on the other by the presence of adults whose experiences have crystallized their thoughts. There must, therefore, be safeguarded the principle of a graded program in the church.

But there are needs, interests, and experiences which children share with adults; and there should be opportunity for meeting these common needs through a common service of worship. The members of the church family live in the same world. And all the members of the church family are children of a common Father upon whom they are all dependent.

Moreover, both adults and children need the sense of fellowship one with the other in worship. For children to see the entire congregation worshiping together, the men of affairs and the humble workers, "bright youth and snow-crowned age," is an experience of high religious value. For adults to see the joyous enthusiasm of the children, to feel the sense of continuity of the fellowship of God's people from age to age, to catch a glimpse of that which shall be when a "loftier race than e'er the world hath known shall rise," is to enrich their own worship.

And so, as a part of the total program of the church for children there may be occasions for a common service of worship for all the members of the church family, planned with all participants in mind. Let us hasten to say that we are not thinking of a special sermonette or service for children interjected into the midst of the adult service. Rather, we are thinking of a service of worship

in which all the members of the church may share together. Clearly, it will require careful planning on the
part of the minister, the choir, and the children's leaders
to make such a service one in which children and adults
alike may really participate. Certain adjustments may
have to be made in the usual order of the church service.
The question is: Is it worth it? There is a growing conviction among church members that occasions when the
entire church family worship together, either as a regular part of the church program or in scheduled special services, are worth what it requires to plan them. They are
worth it because of what such an experience contributes to
the boys and girls in their own religious experiences and
because it helps them to come to a growing appreciation
of the church as the *church* and a deepening understanding of the significance in the earth of the world community
of Christians.

In Spirit and in Truth

Worship may be a retreat from life, an escape from the
necessity of facing, and dealing with, its problems. Sometimes it may be, as Amos and Isaiah pointed out long
ago, a substitute for true religion. But such worship is
not the worship of the God of our Lord Jesus Christ. Such
worship is not *Christian* worship. For Christian worship
requires that we draw near to God in the spirit of Jesus,
making our prayers and presenting our gifts and offering
our praise in his name. In his name we cannot ask for
ourselves exemption from struggle or suffering; in his
name we cannot retreat from the high demand that we
be children of God in the midst of a crooked and perverse
generation; in his name we cannot substitute beautiful
ceremonies for courageous devotion to the will of God.

In his name we may draw near to God in complete

assurance that he is drawing near to us, seeking us, supporting us, helping us. In his name we may pray for the triumph of righteousness, knowing that righteousness will triumph. In his name we may offer our lives to God to use as he will, knowing full well that we shall then find life full of joy and peace and confidence.

And thus we may help our children to worship God in spirit and in truth.

The FAITH of
OUR CHILDREN

MARY ALICE JONES

Some of the Questions Which This Book Considers: How can we help our children to think intelligently and reverently about how they came to be? How can we lead them to sense their relation to God? How can we teach them to give as well as to receive love? How can we meet the problems of suffering and disaster in terms which a child can understand? What shall we say to children when they ask us why the wicked prosper while the righteous suffer? How may we make Jesus real to boys and girls? What shall we say to their questions about the future life? What does it really mean to be good? How can we use the Bible in furthering the religious growth of children? What shall we teach them about the Church? How may the Church become a spiritual home for growing boys and girls? How can we teach them to pray? How may we help them to worship God in spirit and in truth?